Move Over, Move Up, *or* Move On

9 Proven Leadership Lessons for Optimal Results

thank you!

Chris Boguslaw, MEd

Chris Boguslaw
"Boosie"

Move Over,
Move Up,
or
Move On

9 Proven Leadership Lessons
for Optimal Results

ISBN: 978-1-7344253-0-7

Credits

Editing:	Positively Proofed
	info@positivelyproofed.com
Design, art direction, and production:	Melissa Farr, Back Porch Creative,
	info@backporchcreative.com

Cover image © istockphoto.com.

Dedication

I dedicate this book to all the managers and employees who show up for work, day in and day out, committed to doing the best job that they can while incorporating kindness, understanding, and – yes – even some accountability. Thanks for giving it your all!

Foreword

Allow me to introduce "Bogie," the main character of *Move Over, Move Up, or Move On.*

If you are reading this book, you're probably a little out of the ordinary, special and unique. You get it. You care about others and see life as a journey. You are always looking for ways to not only improve yourself but also for opportunities to help others. You are a lifelong learner, just like Bogie.

You know there is no "end game" but rather a continuous spectrum of opportunities to volunteer, help, assist, improve … (You can finish the rest of this sentence with whatever adjectives you would like and whatever projects you are working on.)

Because of your outlook and your choices, you are doing your best to make a difference in others' lives. And, trust me, you are making a difference. Every kind smile, helpful gesture, selfless action means something. You may not realize it right now, but trust me, kindness is always recognized and appreciated.

We all have a little "Bogie" in each of us. "Bogie" by "Bogie," we can join forces to collectively make a positive difference in the lives of others. Of course, we stumble, fall, and make poor decisions along the way, but like Bogie, we keep getting up, brushing ourselves off, and trying to do better.

Each of us brings different experiences to the table, and these scenarios have shaped us into who we are. Now let's see what makes our main character, Bogie, tick.

First-grade Redux Bogie – Don't make 'failure' a big deal

As Bogie entered his familiar first-grade classroom for the second year in a row, he couldn't have been more excited to see Sister Anthony again. It was a long summer break, and he was excited to see his friends. Sister Anthony was, as always, all smiles and welcomed Bogie with a hug and kindness. As Bogie took his seat, everything was the same except his friends from last year were replaced with new faces. Bogie found it odd that he had seen his friends from last year in the hall as they were arriving, but they all went into another classroom. At six years old, not overanalyzing things is truly a gift and a lesson that we as adults sometimes lose along the way.

It wasn't until one of Bogie's friends from the previous year mentioned to him at the end of the week that Bogie had "flunked." This explained why he wasn't in second grade with everyone else. Whoa, this caught Bogie off guard. Up until this point, Bogie was so excited because he thought he was the luckiest kid in the school. You see, in 6-year-old Bogie's mind, he thought he must have been special to continue to be permitted to stay in first grade. He just assumed he would stay there for the next eight years. By then, he would know everyone in the school! How cool is that?!?

That evening, Bogie told his parents what his friend had said about him "flunking" first grade. Their reply was, as always, a textbook lesson in how to not exaggerate and overanalyze things. Bogie's parents simply said that he didn't flunk but rather was held back because "you liked to play too much and never did your homework." That was true, and there were plenty of times Bogie's parents tried to work with him to finish his schoolwork. Again, at six years old, our Bogie was more interested in recess and playing than schoolwork.

Without making a big deal of it, Bogie's parents and teachers taught him:

- ⊃ There are consequences to our actions, or lack of action.

- ⊃ Failures or setbacks don't have to define us. Instead of dwelling on such setbacks, they should instead be learning experiences.

- ⊃ Sometimes some of us just need more time to develop "buy in."

- ⊃ Always look for the positive takeaways. Bogie met more friends during that extra year of first grade. To this day, they are still in his life. Looking back, Bogie realizes that Sister Anthony, the school, and his parents did him a "solid" by giving him the gift of repeating first grade.

Class-Clown Bogie – It's all fun and games until someone gets hurt

Bogie was never a good primary or secondary student. He focused on the social aspects of school. He loved seeing his friends, the teachers, bus drivers, and the office, janitorial and cafeteria staff. While Bogie was never disruptive, he never applied himself to his studies. Sure, the teachers tried to stress the importance of his schoolwork, but Bogie didn't listen. Long story short, Bogie made it through school but found limited post-secondary educational opportunities. Again, Bogie found himself learning more valuable lessons:

- People progress through life. While they may like you and wish nothing but the best for you, they will pursue their own path. If we don't progress, we limit ourselves and will complete the journey being known as "that guy."

- Well-run institutions/organizations are perfectly aligned to achieve their mission. School's primary mission is to educate students. While Bogie may have been well liked among his classmates, the educators and staff only had so much time to allocate to him. He learned that the mission must come first. It's "nothing personal" that people have jobs to do and can't focus on the class clown. Don't get in the way of others doing their job.

- Sometimes we don't get a "do over." As Bogie approached the end of his senior year, he realized that he wouldn't get a second chance to improve his grades. That ship had sailed and the consequences of not applying himself were irreversible. His final high school transcript was indeed just that: FINAL.

- Most importantly, Bogie learned that childhood was for children. Never lose sight of your own responsibility to grow.

U.S. Army Bogie – Seize opportunities to reinvent yourself

Bogie was extremely fortunate to finally have learned from his high school mistakes. He made a commitment to himself, as the U.S. Army recruitment poster exclaims, to "be all he could be." Two months after graduation, Bogie joined the military and found a place where he could thrive.

While he knew the Army wasn't his ultimate career choice, he committed to be the best soldier he could be. He did what he was asked, studied what he needed to, and volunteered for various missions and assignments. To his surprise, all of his positive actions were met with not only recognition but also reward. During his three-year enlistment, Bogie received several medals and promotions, and he made numerous friends. More importantly, he matured. He found that you can still be serious while not taking yourself too seriously. Also, when you are responsible for doing something, you need to do everything in your power to do the best job you can. Bogie learned:

- ◌ High-performing teams must focus on the assigned mission, which must be clear and understood by all.

- ◌ Clear communication, roles and responsibilities, and commitment to self, team, and mission are foundational components of high-performing individuals and teams.

- ◌ Organizations must have a reward structure to recognize achievements beyond what is expected.

- ◌ We can achieve more than we ever thought possible. We need to maintain a positive outlook and surround ourselves with leaders, mentors, family, and friends, who not only care about us but also push us to achieve our potential. Probably most importantly, we need to be courageous enough to take the first step and seek guidance from others, ask for assistance when needed, and always be open to learning.

- ◌ Leaders and team members both have HUGE responsibilities.

  - ➡ Leadership or "rank" is a responsibility to live up to. Leaders are responsible for not only their own actions but also for others' actions and lives. Leaders must be

100% committed to leading others in an honorable way.

→ Team members must recognize that their job is to support the leadership team and their team members, and to follow through on assignments.

⟳ Last, and most importantly, Bogie learned about people, specifically those from different cultures and with diverse backgrounds. He learned that people are people, and respect and kindness are universal languages. If we enter each relationship with a focus on respect and being kind, it's amazing what we can learn.

Of course, there is so much more to Bogie and his story. To find out – well, that's what *Move Over, Move Up, or Move On* is all about! Enjoy the story. Once you've finished, you can be a "Bogie," too. Learn more at www.teambogie.com.

Table of Contents

Introduction   13
Betting on Leadership

Chapter One   23
Consistency and Commitment – Foundational Building
Blocks of Leadership

Chapter Two   35
Be the Employee You'd Want Reporting to You

Chapter Three   51
Listen, Value, Lead – Team Performance and
the Power of Awareness

Chapter Four   61
One Last Round of Yuenglings – Assembling a
Winning Team

Chapter Five   75
LVL Leadership IRL (In Real Life) – Acting on Team
Feedback

Chapter Six   97
Team Synergy – Everyone Contributes

Chapter Seven   105
The Role of Delegation – Developing Future Leaders

Chapter Eight   115
The Boss Is On Line 1 – Honoring Confidentiality

Chapter Nine   121
Move Over, Move Up, or Move On – Pushing the Ball
Forward

About the Author   128

Acknowledgments   129

About Team Bogie   130

Introduction

Betting on Leadership

For someone like me, hotel pubs were all too familiar territory. This one was called The Las Vegas Lounge, but the locals always referred to it as The LVL. There wasn't anything special about The LVL. In fact, it was pretty much a carbon copy of the hundreds of other pubs I've unwound in over the course of my career – not very busy, dimly lit, and it had the standard beer smell that sticks to your clothes long after you've left. But, hey, happy hour lasted for another 30 minutes, so I was eager to grab a seat.

It was Monday evening and I was in town to facilitate a weeklong strategic planning session for a Fortune 500 client and its management team. I thought tonight's dinner would be like all the others. Basically, when dining alone on business trips, I liked to locate the most inconspicuous table, where I could eat my dinner and not offend anyone by taking a call from home to catch up on everything I was missing. When the elusive "private/quiet" table wasn't available, then I'd grab a bite at the bar.

That was where I decided to sit tonight, even though there were tables available. I wasn't sure what prompted me to break with my business trip routine, but that small random choice was about to change my life.

I plopped down at the far end of the bar and waved a little to get Maya the bartender's attention.

"Hi, what can I get you?" she said, smiling.

"I'll have a Yuengling®, please," I said.

Maya told me that she had Bud Light on special for happy hour – two bucks a pop – but I respectfully declined.

"Thanks for the heads up, but I'm loyal to Yuengling," I replied.

She didn't ask me why, but I believed I needed to explain anyway.

"Did you know that Yuengling is America's oldest brewery? And it's from my home state of Pennsylvania, and damn it, that means something to me."

I saw a momentary spark of interest in Maya's eyes, but it was fleeting.

"Bottle or draft?" Maya asked. Her eyes were glued to her phone and she seemed preoccupied with whatever she was looking at.

I could see she didn't feel like chatting it up, so I quietly responded, "Draft, please."

From somewhere in what seems to be my diminishing stored memory, a thought crept into my mind and I chuckled to myself.

Over thirty-plus years ago, as a slick-sleeve private standing guard duty in West Germany during the Cold War, I made a vow to always order draft beer over bottled/canned beer. It was one of those promises a kid makes to himself when staring down the responsibilities of adulthood for the first time. At least when life got tough, I could always enjoy a nice, cold glass of beer.

But it was a while before I had the chance to enjoy the one I'd just ordered. Maya was very distracted while pouring my beer, pausing to check her phone every so often. I couldn't help but think how that damn phone was probably ruining her tips! But as soon as that negative thought came into my mind, something sparked inside of me. I almost flinched. I wasn't quite sure what was compelling me to do this, but I pulled out a pen and jotted down on the paper napkin in front of me:

While first impressions are extremely important, remember to always reserve judgment of others and allow for the "gift of time" to do its job.

Just then, Maya appeared with my Yuengling and a menu. She went over the happy hour specials, and then suddenly she was apologizing to me.

"I'm sorry I keep checking my phone. I'm on leave from school and relocated back home temporarily to help take care of my mother, so I'm texting a lot with my family."

I tried to tell her it was okay and I understood, but from the strained look on her face, she seemed to be having a hard time accepting my forgiveness.

"There's no excuse for using my phone when I'm with customers. Again, I'm sorry."

"Honestly, it's all good. Thanks for sharing your story with me." Since she still looked a little weary, I decided to go a little further.

"For what it's worth, I'm really impressed with your decision to take on such an important task. I know it can't be easy, but trust me. When we do the right thing, everything else eventually falls into place."

"Thanks, that's nice of you to say." Maya's eyes seemed to brighten a little and she left me with the menu, moving on to tend to another customer.

I looked down at the napkin again and, for some reason I couldn't explain, I wrote down some more notes.

Revealing personal information takes courage, but it also allows for increased understanding and improved communication.

I wasn't sure why I even bothered to look at a menu when I was eating alone, because I always ordered the same thing when I traveled. I treated myself to a burger and fries on the first day. For the rest of the week, it was a big salad and some form of protein. But today was burger and fries, and my stomach was rumbling, so I was ready for whatever greasy goodness The LVL served.

Out of the blue, the guy sitting next to me struck up a conversation.

"Couldn't help but overhear your conversation before. Gotta admire Maya for how she handled things just now."

"Totally agree," I said.

We briefly made some small talk about the local sports teams, and after a few minutes, he commented on the way I ordered my beer.

"Listen, I like Yuengling as much as the next person, but it was what you said about being loyal to their brand that intrigued me."

"Really, why?" I asked.

"Well, I see the importance of loyalty, but to be honest, I don't think the majority of employers do. Managers say they want employees to be happy, motivated, and…" Then he paused for a moment, like he was trying to remember something. "What's the latest buzzword? Oh, right. *Engaged.* My boss wants me and my team to be engaged, but his actions say otherwise."

He had more venting to do, but he stopped himself, probably because he didn't want to scare me off. But as an organizational development and performance improvement consultant – which is basically a fancy way of saying that I am someone who works with individuals and teams to improve communications, accountability, and motivation – I was definitely interested in hearing more of what he had to say.

So I extended my hand and introduced myself.

"Hi, I'm Peter, but please call me Bogie. It's a pleasure to meet you."

He shook my hand and smiled. "Justin Hernandez. The pleasure is all mine." We both took a sip of beer and then he said, "Bogie. Interesting name. Are you a golfer?"

I laughed a little because I get asked this A LOT.

"I enjoy playing a round or two of golf, but it's not really my thing. Bogie is a nickname that goes way back to elementary school and it kind of stuck. And it's Bogie with an 'ie,' not a 'y.'"

We talked a little bit about ourselves – where we were from, our lines of work, stuff like that – and then Maya came back, took our orders, and went about her business.

I leaned toward Justin and said, "Maya is an impressive kid. She's going to achieve whatever she wants to in life."

Justin replied, "Yes, first rate for sure."

"So how long are you in town for?" I asked him.

"A week. I'm here for a corporate retreat."

"Cool. You excited?"

Justin rolled his eyes. "Not really. If my team's performance doesn't improve soon, I have a strong feeling they're going to let me go."

"Sorry to hear that," I said, feeling bad that Justin wasn't in a good place at work.

"What about you? Why are you here?" Justin seemed eager to shift the focus away from himself, so I went with the flow.

"I'm here for a corporate retreat, too, but for a different organization. I've been working with this client for over ten years now."

"Whoa. That's a long time. You must really like it," he said.

"Yeah, I do."

"Why is that?" Justin asked.

"Well, this client really invests in their employee and leadership development programs. They have these biannual strategic planning sessions that include various exercises that focus on the foundational building blocks of good self- and group leadership."

Justin raised his eyebrows and smirked. "Foundational building blocks, huh?"

"Yeah, I know it sounds cheesy. But in my experience, those are the tried-and-true leadership skills, like communication, self-discipline, accountability, reward, commitment, interpersonal skills, recognition, and so on. They've always separated high-achieving individuals and organizations from the ones that don't last."

"Those skills are just based on common sense and intuition, though," Justin argued.

"I don't quite see it that way. I believe these skills are something that you build, and when you do the work, it changes everything."

Justin was giving me a blank stare, so I gave him an example.

"It's kind of like exercising. We know it's good for us, but when we see the benefits from our efforts, we tend to stick with it and make it part of our routine."

I knew our meals would be arriving soon, and while I was enjoying talking shop with Justin, once my burger and fries came, I'd naturally lose my focus. (Who wouldn't?)

So I extended an offer to Justin.

"Hey, since we're going to be here over the next few days, I'd like to make you a wager."

"Let's hear it," Justin said.

"Why don't we meet at The LVL every night this week, and I'll tell you what I think the most important leadership traits are and how to master them. If after the end of our meetings you still think it's all common sense and not something you have to consciously practice, the dinners are on me. If you come around, I'll still pay for the dinners, but all that I ask is that you pay it forward by sharing these leadership lessons with someone else."

"That's a hard deal to turn down," Justin said. "But please, allow me to pay for the meals. You might think this is weird, but … I don't think it was an accident that we wound up sitting next to each other tonight. If I have to look for a new job soon, I'll need all the help I can get!"

As soon as Justin and I shook hands, our juicy burgers were placed in front of us, and boy did they look good.

Bogie's Notes

➲ Try not to jump to conclusions. First impressions aside, others' true character takes time to surface. Allow for the Gift of Time.

➲ Sharing personal information increases understanding and improves communication between colleagues.

➲ Tried-and-true leadership skills separate high-achieving individuals and organizations from those who are destined to fail.

➲ Leaders must invest in themselves so they are strong enough – physically, mentally, and spiritually – to lead others.

chapter one

Consistency and Commitment

Foundational Building Blocks of Leadership

The next day, I was excited to have dinner with Justin and find out how his day went at the retreat. I was also a little worried he might reconsider the whole deal and not show up. Had I crossed a line, acting as though I had all the answers? Was he just being nice when he accepted my offer?

There was only one way to find out.

When I arrived at The LVL, Justin wasn't anywhere to be found. A prickle of embarrassment crept up my neck when I grabbed a seat at the bar, but I tried to put it out of my mind. Even if he didn't show, it was nice to have some company last night.

I said hello to Maya, who was wiping down the countertop with a rag. When she saw me, she smiled and nodded, pouring me a Yuengling right from the draft, without even having to ask.

Yep, this kid was totally on the ball.

"Hey, thanks for remembering," I said when Maya slid the beer in front of me.

As Maya continued to clean the bar, she smiled again and said, "I know, all things being equal, why would anyone ever order anything but a draft?"

We both laughed.

I took a sip and asked, "So how's your mom doing? A little better, I hope."

"Thanks for asking. Yesterday was a good day," she replied. "My mom has diabetes and she recently had kidney surgery. She's recovering at home now, and some days are better than others, but she's getting stronger and stronger."

"I'm sorry that she's not well, but she'll pull through. I bet she's a tough lady," I said.

"Tougher than most," Maya replied. "Hey, I don't want to sound like I was eavesdropping, but I couldn't help but overhear parts of your conversation with Justin yesterday. I'm studying management and leadership at school. Do you think you'd mind giving me some tips, too?"

"Of course. I already started making some notes from our conversation. Want to take a look?" I reached into my jacket pocket and pulled out the crumpled-up napkin I'd been writing on, and Maya chuckled.

"This isn't exactly legible," she said, squinting her eyes.

"My handwriting is kind of terrible," I said.

"Why don't you use the notes app on your phone? Probably a lot easier and there's less of a chance you'll lose it," Maya suggested.

"Great idea," I said, pulling my phone out and double tapping on the notes app. "Millennials, man. You guys are sharp."

"I can't tell if you're mocking me or not," Maya said, crossing her arms.

"Nah, Bogie isn't the mocking type," a voice from behind me said.

I turned around and saw Justin walking toward the barstool next to me. I smiled, quietly breathing a small sigh of relief.

"If you say so." Maya put a round coaster on the bar in front of Justin, who sat down wearily, like he'd had a long day. "What'll it be?"

"That a Yuengling draft?" he asked me.

"Absolutely," I said.

He drummed his fingers on the bar and said, "I guess it will be the drink of choice for the week."

Once Maya hooked Justin up with a beer, he untucked his buttoned-up shirt and groaned. While I was happy to be hanging out with him again, he seemed to have the weight of the world on his shoulders.

"Things are not off to a good start," he said.

"Sorry to hear that, man," I said. "What happened?"

"Well, there was an important meeting at the beginning of the retreat," Justin explained. "I wanted to make sure I was prepared to talk about the day's agenda. I woke up really early to review sales data and product info. But I totally lost track of time and showed up at the meeting about 15 minutes late."

"Listen, things like that happen to everyone. Most of the time people understand," I said.

"My boss was upset. I could tell." Justin took a big gulp of Yuengling and sighed. "But you know what? It was only 15 minutes. The team was still mingling and getting coffee. It wasn't a big deal."

"That's true. But at the end of the day, if we want people to respect us, we have to hold ourselves accountable," I said. "Justin, you knew you were going to be late. You could have called or emailed your boss to tell him. Or you could have explained when you saw him at the meeting, right?"

Justin nodded. "I guess. Sometimes it just seems easier to let it slide, though. And it's not like I'm late all the time."

"Sure, but easy doesn't always help you in the long run, and if you ask me, consistency is one of the most important foundational blocks of leadership," I said. "Wanna know why?"

Justin signaled for Maya to bring a menu. "Hold on, let me order and then I'll be all ears."

Once Maya sent our orders to the kitchen, I felt that spark of inspiration I experienced last night. All of these ideas started popping into my head. Justin, thankfully, seemed eager to listen.

"The way I see it, **great leaders are all dependable**. No matter where you are on the company food chain, knowing that you can consistently rely on your manager to come through is what makes people feel confident enough to do their jobs well," I said.

"Yeah, but I know plenty of dependable people who wouldn't make great leaders. That can't be all it takes," he replied.

"Of course not. But you can't deny that being consistent and reliable helps people to believe in and trust you, right?" I asked.

"Right," Justin said, nodding in agreement.

"Okay, now, think about every time you board a plane and the flight attendants go through the safety instructions. Why is it that in the event there is a loss of cabin pressure and the oxygen masks deploy, the attendants always tell you to put your mask on first before you provide assistance to those seated around you?"

Justin thought carefully for a moment, and then said, "Well, I had never really paid that much attention to those safety briefings. Thinking about it now, I can see how it is important to put your oxygen mask on before helping someone else, because you can't help anyone if you're dead."

I laughed. "Exactly! Leaders are accountable and responsible for helping others, and the only way they can do it for the long haul is to **invest in themselves**, making sure they're physically, mentally, and spiritually strong and alert."

"That makes sense, but what does it have to do with consistency?" Justin asked.

"Because when it comes to any aspect of your health, *halfway* and *sometimes* aren't enough," I explained. "You have to be fully committed. And as you know, **commitment** is a huge part of being consistent."

Justin glared at me in a semi-joking way. "You're going to make me regret ordering the barbecue ribs, aren't you?"

I laughed again. I really liked his sense of humor.

"Maybe, but that's not my intention, I swear," I said.

"Okay, carry on," said Justin.

At first, I started talking about **committing to exercising**. I definitely wasn't a star athlete or someone who went overboard with exercise. Justin seemed to be in decent shape, too. But I reminded him that, especially with a desk job, sitting down all day wasn't great for our bodies. We were made to move. I told him that before I started running regularly, I went to my doctor for a health assessment, and then I told him I was hoping to run a 5k in a few months. Together we created a solid exercise plan. Having that goal ahead of me really kept me motivated in my workout routines.

"Routine. That's a word that sticks out to me," Justin said.

"Really? Why?"

"Coming up with routines definitely helps to create habits, and habits are another form of—"

"Consistency!" I shouted, pumping a fist into the air.

Justin clapped me on the back and said, "I think the whole bar heard you."

"Sorry. I can be a little excitable. It's a Bogie thing."

"Got it," he said, smiling.

Next we talked about committing to eating healthier. Any doctor or diet book will explain what the benefits of a proper diet are, but when you're making healthy choices, your body will show you how much better off you are. I told Justin I still splurge a little with a burger once a week, but the rest of the time I eat salads, vegetables, lean meats, and fish. I have a lot more energy than I thought possible and it's definitely helped me stay fresh on the job.

"Sometimes I wish I was still in my teens and early twenties. Then I could eat whatever I wanted," I said.

"I'm not looking forward to my metabolism slowing down," Justin replied.

"Hate to break it to you, buddy, but it's going to happen. There is no sense in pretending otherwise," I said, chuckling. "Might as well get a jump on it now."

"What about the beer, though? How many calories is in one Yuengling?" he asked.

"Zero!" I joked.

Justin laughed. "That's a relief!"

The last thing we talked about was being **committed to being grateful**.

"Justin, remember our discussion yesterday about loyalty?" I asked him.

"Yes, I do," he said.

"True leaders care about others and value their loyalty."

"But how do they earn it?" Justin asked curiously. "That's what I'd like to know."

"Would it freak you out if I said deepening their spiritual health?" I replied.

I could see Justin squirming on his barstool a little. I thought he might be afraid that I was going to start preaching to him – not about business but about my religious beliefs.

"I wouldn't be freaked out," he said after a beat or two of silence. "But I do think spirituality is a personal, private thing."

I nodded my head. "I totally hear you. While I am committed to my personal religious faith and beliefs, that is not what I am referring to right now."

"Oh, okay." Justin seemed to ease up a bit.

"The way I see it, spiritual health drives a leader's decisions and actions, and if your actions are congruent with integrity and honor, loyalty will follow. Have you ever been fortunate enough to work for a leader whom you thought the world of?"

Justin immediately smiled. "I've had a few great managers, but there was one whom I really admired: my former boss Christine. Everyone in our division respected and liked her. She even enjoyed mentoring junior staff."

"Wow. Some managers don't make time for that. You're really lucky to have worked with such a great leader," I said.

"I know. I was pretty disappointed when she left."

"So what made Christine an exceptional manager? Maybe we could make a list," I suggested, pulling out my phone and opening the notes app, just like Maya recommended.

With no hesitation, Justin went on to describe Christine's management/leadership style with ease. As Justin was talking, I jotted down the adjectives he used to describe her, my fingers typing as fast as they could.

➡ Disciplined
➡ Caring
➡ Compassionate
➡ Humble
➡ Patient
➡ A sense of personal accountability/responsibility
➡ Forgiving
➡ Knowledgeable
➡ Developed others
➡ Held others accountable
➡ Confident

When Justin finished, I mentioned that many of the traits he identified are associated with someone who is spiritually healthy. Great leaders know this, and that's why they incorporate them into a daily practice where other people are prioritized and someone else's desires are seen as just as important as their own.

I told Justin that I have worked with numerous individuals and teams who were committed to improving their own or their team's performance. Of the traits he identified, the one thing that remains a constant is *caring*. Your colleagues want to know that you care about them.

"That's really true," Justin said.

"And that's what breeds loyalty," I replied. "If someone knows you care about them, they are free to focus on their job. They feel valued and secure in their position. And they want to do their best work."

Justin thought for a second and replied, "You make a really good point there."

Maya came by with our food, setting down a salad in front of me and a ribs and french fries entrée in front of Justin. "Enjoy, guys," she said.

Just as she was about to walk away, Justin called out for her to wait.

"Do you think you could take mine back to the kitchen and put in an order for a salad instead?" he asked.

"Is something wrong with it?" she asked.

Justin just grinned and said, "I'm considering making a big commitment."

"To ... lettuce?" she said, confused.

I raised my beer glass, signaling a toast. "To leadership!"

Justin clinked his glass against mine while Maya grabbed his plate with a smile.

Bogie's Notes

⊃ Great leaders are consistent, dependable, and hold themselves accountable.

⊃ When workers trust and believe in their leaders, it frees them up to concentrate on excelling in their job.

⊃ While true leaders value loyalty, their employees just want a leader who cares.

chapter two

Be the Employee You'd Want Reporting to You

On Wednesday evening, I headed down to The LVL a little early. I was hoping to catch up with Maya to see how her mother was recovering from her surgery. Much to my surprise, Justin was already there, chatting with her.

They both smiled, pointing to a beer that they had waiting for me.

"I hope you don't mind, but I had such a great day, I couldn't wait to get here to tell you about it," Justin said. "I was about to give Maya the play-by-play when you walked in."

"My shift doesn't start for a few minutes," Maya added. "Do you mind if I join you guys?"

"Mind? Not at all, I think it is great," I replied, thinking I should have tried to involve Maya sooner. Then again, Maya was showing a lot of initiative right now and I really admired that quality.

I reached for my phone and quickly typed up another note to myself:

A great leader doesn't wait to be offered a seat at the table; they ask for the opportunity.

"So how's your mom doing, Maya?" I asked.

"She's giving diabetes hell right now," she said, laughing a little. "Each day is better than the one before."

"That's great news," I said.

"It is," Maya said. "Hopefully I'll be gone in a couple of weeks. Not to sound like a nerd, but I really miss school."

"Your education is extremely important, and once you earn your degree, it's one of those things that can never be taken away from you. It will benefit you for the rest of your life," Justin said, which put a smile on Maya's face.

"So tell us about your day already," Maya said to Justin.

"Okay. Bogie, you're going to love this," he said. "This morning I forced myself to get out of bed at 5 a.m. and went straight to the hotel gym."

"Wow! That's awesome," I said, impressed.

"Yeah, well, at first I didn't feel so awesome. I was pretty tired. But after I walked on the treadmill for thirty minutes, I had a lot of energy. I also felt more positive, too."

Maya nodded. "I know what you mean. I jog a couple of times a week, and if I don't, it totally affects my mood."

"For breakfast, I had oatmeal and fruit instead of my usual bacon, egg, and cheese sandwich," Justin said.

"Good call," I said.

"Then I got to my seminar ten minutes early and spent the whole day focusing on being the type of employee I'd like to have reporting to me," he said.

"Very cool," I said. "But I'm curious why that was important to you."

"Well," Justin said, "I would be lying if I didn't tell you that our meeting yesterday shook me up a bit. We only had one dinner and I was already getting kind of anxious about all the things in my life I'd have to do differently. When I got back to my room, I thought to myself, "*Is change worth all the effort?*" Also, for some reason I was worried about letting you down, which is weird because I barely know you and —"

"Hold on a second," I interrupted. "The person you need to worry about disappointing is yourself, not me or anyone else. And I get that change can be scary, but the key is to remember that it doesn't have to happen overnight."

"That's true," Maya chimed in. "And the cool thing is, you're challenging yourself, even though it's not easy. That takes a lot of courage."

"Couldn't agree more," I added. "Sorry I got us off track. Justin, why did you decide to try to become the employee you'd want reporting to you?" I asked.

"Because after I read through the notes from our meeting, I could see there were so many areas where I could be doing better," he explained. "I just felt like I owed it to myself and the people who worked with me to start living up to a higher standard. Besides, I can't complain about management not being fully invested in their teams when I wasn't fully invested in mine, either."

"Be the change you wish to see in the world," Maya said in almost a whisper.

"I love that quote," I said. "Gandhi, right?"

"Yep. It's one of my favorites," she replied. "I actually have a notebook where I write down inspirational quotes. Every time I need a boost of positivity, all I have to do is get out a pen and inscribe some new ones on the pages. I instantly feel better."

"Okay, that's amazing," I said. "I think I'm going to try that."

"Me, too," Justin added. "Anyway, before everyone else showed up to the seminar, I told myself that for the next few days, I'm going to try my very best and follow Bogie's advice. I also jotted down the following things that I wanted to focus on."

Justin showed Maya and me the list he'd written on his phone:

1. Actively participate
2. Be positive
3. Volunteer

"Nice!" Maya said.

I nodded. "Volunteering is a great idea, too."

"Thanks. I gotta admit, knocking the chip off my own shoulder was long overdue. I had this sense of empowerment that I hadn't felt for a long time. It was as if the moment I took control of my actions, I felt stronger and more confident. I even spoke up in the seminar and shared some ideas, which I rarely do."

"That's amazing. Did anyone else notice how much more engaged you were?" I asked.

He shrugged. "No, not at first. But at the end of the day, my manager told me that the senior leadership team really liked my suggestions. They want to hear more about them."

"How awesome," I said.

"I think your advice and coaching was just the boost I needed."

"I'm so glad to hear that."

Justin raised his glass and all three of us clinked them together in congratulations.

After I had another sip of beer, I asked, "So, are you both ready for tonight's lesson?"

Suddenly an alarm sounded and Maya reached for her phone. Once she looked at it, she sighed. "Damn. My shift is about to start. Don't forget to take notes, you guys."

"You got it," I said.

"You're really nice for doing this, Bogie," she replied.

"Thanks, but honestly I'm only paying it forward. Just like my mentor asked me to when he helped me years ago."

As Maya walked away, she turned a little bit and asked over her shoulder, "You want menus?"

"No, we'll just go with what we had yesterday," Justin replied, and Maya disappeared behind the kitchen door.

"Well, it sounds like you had a great day," I said.

"I did. Let's keep it going. What's the topic for tonight?"

"Team performance. Tell me, what are things like back at the office?"

Justin replied, "I really have a great group of folks on the team. Sure, some are stronger than others. But overall, we work well together. Although turnover seems to be a growing problem, but I think that's because the economy has been picking up."

"True, a good economy certainly does lead to more opportunity for staff, but it's usually not the only reason," I said. "Maybe we could make a list of the last three employees who left and what the circumstances were."

"Good idea. That way we can see if there is anything they have in common," Justin said.

"Exactly. There could be some invisible factors in play."

As Justin gave me the details, I recorded them all on my phone, creating a rough chart.

Employee departures over the past nine months

Name	Years With Company	Job Performance Rating (Scale 1 to 5)	Description / Comments	Reason Given for Leaving	Rehire (Y/N?) Why
Colin	6	3	Knowledgeable, reliable, polite, professional. He could have excelled, but he didn't seem that excited about or committed to the job.	Start his own software business	No. Not committed.
Aimee	3	5	Committed, hard worker, resourceful, great analytical skills, team player, great computer skills.	Career growth	Yes. Aimee advanced the division with Improved processes. Great attitude, creative, self-starter. Great employee.
Jim	4	5	Quiet, more reserved than Colin and Aimee, but extremely talented at anticipating senior leadership's needs. Hard working, committed, smart, great at data mining and programming.	Career growth	Yes. Good fit for the team. Always willing to assist. Great employee.

When we finished, I said, "Okay, Justin, can you describe how you managed Colin, Aimee, and Jim?"

"Like everyone else," he replied.

"You're sure you didn't treat them any differently than the staff who stayed?"

"I don't think so," he said. "Actually, I thought of them and few others on my staff as high achievers. Essentially they were my 'go-to' people. I would often give them the assignments that were the most challenging and they never failed to deliver. They came to the senior staff meetings. The leadership team thought of them practically as management. So when they left, a big void formed and I'm still struggling to fill it."

"No one has assumed their responsibilities?" I asked.

"Not yet. Their departures really caught me off guard. I had no clue that they would leave."

"Got it. Okay, the next step is to look at the remaining employees on the team." Justin nodded. He talked while I wrote down some more notes.

Current Team Members

Name	Years With Company	Job Performance Rating (Scale 1 to 5)	Strengths	Growth Opportunities	Recommend for Advancement (Yes/No)
Jayden	7	5	Dependable, extremely knowledgeable, recognized expert in his area of responsibility.	Better time management, leadership training.	Yes
Bodhi	20	4	Well liked, good at assigned duties.	Stronger analytical skills.	No. Not interested in career development/ advancement.
Mitch	3	4	Dependable, committed, good at assigned duties.	Needs to learn more about the organization.	No. Has the potential, but is not willing.
Gwen	12	5	Hard worker, committed, good at assigned duties.	Needs to learn more analytical skills and about the organization.	No. Needs more analytical skills and leadership training.

"All right, Justin," I began after I reviewed my notes, "in my experience, when looking back and analyzing staff departures, there are almost always clues that people are considering leaving. I don't pretend to know all the reasons your employees moved on, but listening to you, I can make a few educated guesses."

"Okay, I'd love to hear them." Justin channeled his attention on me, so I could tell he was really interested in hearing my general assessment.

"I am a firm believer that in most cases, if an employee is talented and doesn't believe in the leadership at their company, they'll realize they have options. They'll most likely leave so they can align themselves with a leader they believe has their best interests in mind."

"So basically you're saying that the one-on-one relationship between manager and employee is more important than the overall culture at the company," Justin said.

"Yep, the overwhelming percentage of the time, that's the reason."

"Okay, then what am I doing wrong?" he asked.

"I think this is a case of performance punishment," I suggested.

Justin squinted at me in a "huh?" kind of way, so I explained further.

"While not intending to, leaders can often punish their top-tier employees by giving them more and more work because they are capable, conscientious, and willing. At the same time, they fail to hold the lower tier accountable for being mediocre at their assigned duties."

Justin's face lit up, like he understood where I was going with this. "It's almost as if those leaders are giving the lower tier a pass."

"Very true," I said.

"Meanwhile, the top tier probably feels resentment for carrying a much bigger workload, which could feel like punishment for being great at their jobs."

"There you go. If you're in the top tier, you can feel taken advantage of if you don't feel valued and seen for the excellence you demonstrate."

"This is really eye-opening," Justin said.

"Okay, now let's talk more about the people who have stayed." I showed Justin the notes that I had taken and pointed out that his entire staff was rated as exceeding performance expectations. However, he indicated that no one stepped up to fill the void from the earlier departures and there was just one employee he viewed as worthy of a promotion.

"Is that another sign of a problem?" he asked.

"Well, when it comes to evaluating performance, managers tend to take the easy way out and inflate the ratings of lesser-performing team members. And, when performance ratings are inflated –"

"Leaders fail to give staff opportunities for growth, development, and advancement," he interjected.

"Absolutely," I said.

"I get it. But everyone on my team is nice and it's hard to be honest in performance assessments. As much as people say they want feedback, what they really want is to be told they're doing a great job and don't need to improve."

"Listen, giving evaluations is super challenging," I replied. "But **a major part of a leader's role is to ensure your team accomplishes the identified goals and objectives.** If you fail to do that, you put your own position at risk and also your department's and possibly the company. Remember, you are evaluating performance, not popularity."

Then I went on to tell him that if evaluations aren't delivered in an objective manner, top performers are left with these three choices:

1. Become disgruntled or disengaged. For various personal reasons, they may choose to continue to work for their manager, but be clear – they are most likely suffering in silence and not delivering their best work.

2. Recognize that high-achieving performance doesn't really matter or get recognized, so they downshift until they meet the lower tier's pace.

3. They will leave. Top-tier staff members are always in demand, so they have options and will pursue them.

"Wow, looks like I've been in denial for some time," Justin said, casting his gaze down into his beer. "I think Jim, Aimee, and Colin left because I failed to hold the whole team accountable to the same standards and never truly rewarded their stellar work, as I should have. I don't think I wanted to admit it, but they left because they were tired of performing above expectations yet being treated the same as everyone else."

"Don't beat yourself up about it," I said. "It's hard to notice these things unless you really examine them."

"So what can I do about it now?"

I was about to respond, but then Justin answered his own question. "I need to meet with the team, listen to them, and open up a dialogue about ways to move forward. I have to make sure that the team knows what's expected and how we need to hold ourselves accountable as individuals, as well as a unit."

"Great idea!" I said, trying to lift his spirits a bit. "I think everyone on your team will appreciate the opportunity."

Justin smiled. "I do, too."

"Can I offer one more suggestion that you might find useful?" I asked.

"Sure, go ahead."

"Okay. In all my years of managing, I focused on four principles."

As I spoke, Justin typed everything out on his phone, word for word.

1. **Creating a Caring Environment** – People want to know that you care about them and their family.

2. **Life Balance** – People want to come to work, know they are appreciated, be set up to succeed, be rewarded, and then they want to go home to their families and loved ones without worrying about the job.

3. **Accountability** – People want everyone to be held accountable for performing their duties. There is nothing more de-motivating than when leaders fail to hold others accountable for their actions or lack of performance.

4. **Reward and Recognition** – You must take the time to find out what motivates people. Once you determine whether it's financial, time, learning opportunities, autonomy, etc., then you need to build your recognition and reward structure around it.

"This is great stuff," Justin said.

As he finished typing, Maya brought our dinners and quickly moved on to another customer. I hadn't noticed, but The LVL had gotten really busy as we were talking. Maya was handling it like a boss, of course.

"You're wishing this salad was a burger, aren't you?" I asked, nudging Justin in the arm. He turned and saw the grin on my face, then laughed.

"It's that obvious?"

"Sorry, I couldn't help but tease you a little bit."

"That's okay. I can take it."

Then we dived into our food and made plans to meet up tomorrow.

Bogie's Notes

⊃ Great leaders constantly seek ways to improve.

⊃ Just because your top performers are your best go-to employees, don't "punish them" with extra work. Never take anyone for granted.

⊃ Good managers take performance evaluations seriously. Cutting your weakest links too much slack often perpetuates peer resentment.

⊃ Don't pigeonhole your staff. Always strive to offer employees room for growth, development, and advancement.

chapter three

Listen, Value, Lead

Team Performance and the Power of Awareness

On Thursday, I met Justin in the hotel lobby. He was excited to bring me up to speed on everything that happened at his retreat, and I was really looking forward to chatting with him. Normally, at this point in my business trip, I start to slow down and drag a bit given how draining all the activity is. But my dinners with Justin were keeping me energized.

I also started compiling notes on my computer as soon as I got back to my room. I even stayed up late the night before, jotting down ideas and things I wanted to chat with Justin about. I got in such a writing groove that I missed my before-bed check-in with my wife, who was very surprised to hear why I hadn't called. I wasn't exactly a night owl at home.

But I couldn't help it. I had so many thoughts racing in my mind and had to channel them right away.

Justin and I strolled into The LVL. Maya was there to welcome us, as usual. She motioned us toward a table near the center of the bar that had a sign on it:

Reserved – Management and Leadership Training

"What do you guys think?" she asked.

"It's awesome," Justin said.

"Totally makes our dinners feel official," I said. "Thanks, Maya."

"No problem," she said. "It's trivia night and the place usually starts to get packed around 8:30, so I figured I'd best grab a seat ahead of time. Do you mind if I join you when my shift ends?"

"Don't mind at all," Justin and I said, practically in unison.

Maya grinned. "Two Yuenglings coming right up. Oh, we have a taco salad on special. Interested?"

"That sounds great," Justin replied.

"Count me in," I said.

We headed over to our table. When we sat down, I asked Justin how his day went.

"Couldn't have gone better. Last night I reviewed my notes from the last two days and created a list of what I wanted to accomplish today ... and the rest of the week," he said cheerfully. "It definitely made me feel like I'm maximizing my time here. Check it out."

Justin pulled a tablet out of his tote bag and showed me his list.

- ➡ Treadmill – 30 minutes; free weights – 10 minutes
- ➡ Breakfast – healthy and increased water intake
  - ⇨ Called home, talked to wife and kids
  - ⇨ Caught up on the news using my favorite new app
- ➡ Made Dr.'s appointment for my physical
- ➡ Reminded myself to stay positive
- ➡ Focus on rewarding performance and non-performance accountability

"That's a great start," I said.

"Thanks. I came to today's seminar early and was prepared and participated. Just like yesterday," he said. "I realize that we've only had a couple of dinners, but things are really beginning to change for me. I'm much more focused on doing the best I can – not only for my company, but also for my team, my family, and myself. For the first time in a long while, I'm beginning to feel good about where I am."

"Congrats, man. That's incredible." It felt great hearing Justin so enthusiastic and raring to go in all aspects of his life – and we'd only been at this for a few days! "Success starts with the awareness of what we should change, but everyone must have the drive or desire to create actual change. All too often we don't take the necessary steps to do what we need to do until we hit rock bottom. When that happens, there are so many more obstacles to overcome. The sooner you start taking those steps, the better."

"So what's the topic of discussion tonight?" Justin asked.

"Team performance," I answered.

He looked at me like I was forgetting something. "Didn't we cover this yesterday?"

"Last night we looked at where your team stands *now*, but tonight we're going to *look ahead* and define the expectations you have for your team," I explained.

"Got it. That makes sense."

"All too often when I am working with clients, the biggest issue that I come across is that not everyone is on the same page," I said.

"That happens quite a bit at the office," Justin added. "I don't think it's always clear what expectations or standards we're trying to meet."

"When was the last time you talked with your staff – both individually or as a team – about goals, making sure everyone is aware of w*hat they need to achieve, why this task is important, and when it needs to be accomplished?*"

Justin thought for a moment while taking a long sip of beer. "Well, we meet twice a year, both as a group and individually, to go over team targets, mid-year reviews, and end-of-year reviews. I also try to make myself available for staff whenever they need me."

"Great. So when you had your last round of performance reviews, was there anyone who was unhappy with their performance rating?"

"Sure, but that's mainly why I tend to inflate the ratings a bit, so it's less of an issue," Justin said, pausing for a beat. "It wasn't an issue for the person's rating I inflated, but apparently it was an issue for my top performers, who left."

"Exactly," I said.

Suddenly Maya appeared and pulled up a chair. "I have a 10-minute break. Okay if I sit in?"

"You got it," I said, smiling. "We just started talking about performance expectations."

"Cool," Maya said. "Hope I didn't interrupt your train of thought."

"Not at all," I said. "So here's the thing: High-performing teams and individuals need to know what's expected of them and how the company defines success. Everyone involved must agree to the strategy put in place so the group achieves their goals together."

Maya squinted at me. It seemed like she was skeptical about what I was saying. "Everyone has to agree? I haven't been in the workforce very long. Sometimes it seems management doesn't care whether or not the staff agrees with them on pretty much anything."

"I know that some employers just want to give orders and have their staff follow, regardless of what they think," I said, "But when there isn't an agreement about how a team is going to accomplish their goals, performance isn't nearly as strong."

"Why do you think that is?" Justin asked.

"Most people don't like feeling dictated to," I said, simply. "And when they aren't being consulted or asked for their input, they don't feel valued."

"And when someone doesn't feel valued, the work always suffers," Maya answered.

"Yep, that's 100 percent right," I said.

"Okay, so what's the best way to roll out goals to the team?" Justin asked.

"In a way that makes them feel involved, too," Maya added.

"Great question," I replied. "I think expectations should be set by the leadership team. They should identify and clearly state realistic and achievable targets for the group."

"What next?" Maya asked.

"Then management decides how the goals will be achieved and who will be responsible for certain tasks," I continued.

"Let me guess," Justin said. "Supervisors are responsible for communicating the goals to the staff, getting them to agree to the plan of attack, and ensuring the work gets completed."

Before I could say anything else, Maya chimed in with an energetic voice. "Which means the staff is responsible for carrying out the work to the satisfaction of all involved."

"You two nailed it," I said, high fiving them like a coach.

"Woohoo!" cheered Maya.

Justin appeared to be lost in thought though.

"Anything wrong?" I asked him.

"Nothing's wrong, but after listening to all this, the confusion on my team is really beginning to make sense now."

"Why is that?"

Maya leaned in as though she was very interested in what he was about to say.

He replied, "Over the last two years, I was never really clear on the direction that our senior leaders wanted us to go in. Because of that, frustration grew on my own team. People we valued greatly left the company."

Maya and I continued to listen as Justin pieced things together.

"If I don't tell my staff what our goals are, why they matter, and what needs to be done to successfully accomplish them, how can I expect them to rise to the occasion and get the job done?"

"Listen, sometimes even when we do explain those things clearly to our employees, as time goes by, the message can get lost in the shuffle while we all focus on our day-to-day tasks," I said.

Maya nodded her head. "That's true. Take my mom's post-op recovery, for example. The doctor and nurses explained everything to us – how much pain she'd be in, what kind of medicine and services she might need, how long it might take to get her back on her feet again. They even wrote all of it down. But after a few days of just doing our daily routines, we'd forget all that information."

"I should check in with my staff a lot more than I do," Justin said, grabbing his phone and typing up some notes with lightning speed. "I need to remind them of our strategy and their role in it a few times a year at the very least. Especially when our plans might be changing. I have to give them the chance to adapt, right?"

"Yes, that's a great idea," I said. "Sometimes there are new developments, and the more transparent you are about what's happening and why, the more agile your team will be."

Maya looked at her phone, too. "Ugh, bad news. Break is over. But the good news is your food is probably ready."

"I'm starving," said Justin. "I'm so much hungrier now that I'm working out."

"I know what you mean," I said. "I ran this morning and ate like a horse for breakfast."

"I better go get your salads then." Maya stood up and went straight for the kitchen.

"So should we stay for trivia night when we finish our dinner?" Justin asked.

I grinned. "Totally! I love trivia night. My brain contains a lot of useless facts that might really come in handy."

"I'll sign us up then. What should our team name be?" he asked.

"How about … LVL. But instead of Las Vegas Lounge, The LVL stands for Listen, Value, Lead!"

Justin laughed and said, "You got it, Bogie."

Bogie's Notes

⊃ Share with teams and individuals the importance of what they're doing, what they're trying to achieve, and when it needs to be accomplished. Get on the same page!

⊃ Managers should set realistic and reachable performance expectations.

⊃ Allowing and valuing team input encourages worker buy-in.

chapter four

One Last Round of Yuenglings

Assembling a Winning Team

Friday night was our last LVL dinner, and sure enough, Justin and Maya were already there. But much to my surprise, two other people had joined them. As I approached the table, Justin and Maya got up to greet me.

"Hey, Bogie," Justin said. "Hope you don't mind, but we brought some guests who are eager to meet you."

"Of course I don't mind. The more the merrier," I said.

"I brought my manager, David," Justin said.

"And my mom is here, too!" Maya said cheerfully.

"Wow. Really?" I could barely contain the excitement in my voice.

"We know it's only been four days, but we've been talking about our dinners and discussions so much that everyone wanted to meet each other," Maya explained.

"That's great," I said. "I can't wait to meet them."

There was an empty chair between a man with salt-and-pepper hair who was wearing a sports coat, and a woman in a wheelchair who was wearing a tracksuit. I sat down and the introductions began.

"Hi there, I'm David Robinson," the man said, shaking my hand. "I've heard a lot about you from Justin."

"Same here. Thanks for coming tonight," I said.

"And I'm Maya's mom, Toni," the woman said, smiling and bowing her head at me.

"I'm so glad you could be here," I said to her. "How are you feeling?"

"Much better than yesterday, and every day before that," she said, grinning.

Maya put her hands on her mother's shoulders. "This is the first time she's been feeling up to going out since her surgery. I wanted her to have the chance to see you before you went home."

"These talks have been really important to Maya. She's been telling me about them all week," Toni said. "Thank you for sharing your wisdom with her."

"The pleasure was all mine. Your daughter and Justin are fantastic people who have so much to offer. I really enjoyed their company this week. I travel a great deal and I usually dine alone or with a colleague. But I am an educator at heart, so talking shop with Justin and Maya has been so much fun."

I looked over to Maya and her mom and said, "Toni, Maya told us how she took a leave of absence from school so she could help you while you recovered. What an admirable thing for her to do, and I'm sure you couldn't be prouder."

Toni's face was beaming as she took one of Maya's hands in hers. "She's an amazing young woman."

"Agreed. And I don't have to tell you that she shows drive and compassion. I have no doubt she will achieve anything she sets her mind to."

Maya smiled and said, "You're all too kind."

Then I turned to David, Justin's manager, and said, "Justin has shared so much with me over the last few days. It sounds like you and your team run a great shop."

"Thanks for saying that," David replied. "Honestly, I was excited to meet the group because of how much change I've seen in Justin these last few days. At our company, we like to believe that our corporate retreats are designed to encourage open dialogue and the sharing of information. However, we've noticed during the last few retreats that there has been less and less conversation. Justin set a great example over the last week in sharing his thoughts, ideas, and frustrations with the team. I was really impressed."

Justin smiled at hearing this praise from his boss. It was hard to believe that earlier in the week he felt like he might get fired—and now his manager was complimenting him so sincerely. What a turnaround!

"Me, too," I said. "Justin has been working hard to make some big changes. And that takes a lot of courage."

"True, and because Justin was willing to speak freely, others soon followed suit. We heard things this week that have never been brought up before," David continued.

"Here's the best part," Justin said. "The CEO approached David this afternoon and asked to pick my brain about why I've been so much more *engaged*."

I thought back to Monday when Justin rolled his eyes when he mentioned that business buzzword. And here he was telling me the CEO noticed him.

"Of course I told him all about LVL Leadership and the dinner conversations we've been having," Justin said. "He was very interested in learning more about what you do."

David nodded. "Yes, we'd really like to know about what services you provide and the programs you facilitate. Maybe we could bring you on for our next retreat."

"That would be incredible, thank you," I said to David.

"Can we set up a time to talk next week?" he asked.

"Absolutely," I said.

Then, David turned to Maya, who had taken a seat at the table. She wasn't wearing the usual black T-shirt and jeans, so it appeared she had the night off.

"Justin told me what a dedicated employee you are," David began. "We're looking for interns, so I'm hoping you might be interested. The local district manager is accepting applications. What do you think? Will you consider applying?"

Maya's eyes widened with surprise. I couldn't have been happier that she received this offer of encouragement. She totally deserved it.

Maya and her mom looked at each other, appearing to silently exchange thoughts. Once Toni nodded at Maya, she turned back to David.

"Mr. Robinson," she started, but then he quickly responded, "Please call me David."

"Okay, David. I really appreciate the vote of confidence, but I promised the bar owner that I would stay on for the next couple of weeks. And then I plan on heading back to school."

David smiled. "I understand. Maybe when the timing is right?"

"Definitely," Maya said.

David pulled out a card from the inside pocket of his jacket. "Here's my contact info. Feel free to contact me anytime."

"Thank you so much," she replied.

Justin clapped a hand on my back. "So, Bogie, we have one more lesson tonight. What are we talking about?"

"The last lesson is on team membership," I said. Then I looked to David and Toni. "Do you mind if I steal Justin and Maya away for a few minutes?"

"Of course not," Toni said. David concurred.

"Before you got here, Toni was telling me she's a retired manager of an insurance company. We have a lot of stories to trade. We'll be fine," he said.

A server came over and took our dinner order, then Maya, Justin, and I made our way over to the bar for one last round of Yuenglings.

"So, the other evening when we discussed performance accountability, we said one of the most important things a manager can do is ensure that he or she holds their employees accountable for their assigned duties and responsibilities," I began. "To ensure performance expectations are met, the manager is responsible for assembling the best team that they can."

"But what if they join a company and their team is already in place?" Maya asked.

"In that case, I think they're responsible for clearly communicating their own performance expectations as well as the team's expectations," Justin chimed in.

"That's right," I said. "In both of those situations, members need to know that their performance matters. You want your team to be recognized as a high-performing, well-run group, where team membership is viewed as both an honor and an achievement. The staff needs to know that they earned their position on the team and that their membership is directly related to their performance."

"Does that mean if someone isn't performing at a high level, they should be let go?" Justin asked.

"Not necessarily," I replied. "There may be times when less-than-acceptable performance will be tolerated because some things are just out of our control. For instance, when employees are struggling with medical issues or dealing with family crises, high-performing teams will rally around their colleague and support them both inside and outside of the workplace. And they will do it gladly, because we all need support sometimes. However, should circumstances change and once a team member is no longer able or willing to perform to the required level of acceptability, you as the leader must assist the team member in getting back on track. If all efforts fail, it is your responsibility to take appropriate action up to and including dismissing them from the company."

"No one said being a leader was easy," Maya said, and Justin gave her a look that signaled he completely agreed.

"Okay, Justin, let's talk a little bit about our discussion the other day about the three vacancies you have. That's three opportunities to strengthen your team. That's three opportunities you have to get some much-needed relief for your current staff, who have been carrying the load since the other employees' departures. That's three opportunities you have to improve the lives of the candidates you'll be selecting. What a huge honor, privilege, and responsibility."

"That's probably why I'm so nervous," Justin admitted.

"Don't be nervous. I'm about to walk you through it," I said.

"Yes, in Bogie we trust!" Maya said, holding up her beer, and we all clinked glasses together ceremoniously.

"The biggest priority is identifying and recruiting not only the most qualified applicant but also the applicant who will best fit into the team's culture," I explained. "Bringing on a new team member is an area where you cannot settle for less. Remember our discussion earlier this week about the most important things high performers want from their supervisor or manager?"

Justin replied, "Yes, they want to be recognized and rewarded for their own performance. They also want others to be held accountable for their performance, too."

"Precisely! This is your chance to reward the members of your staff by ensuring you are selecting people who will complement the team. Now, let's talk about how to go about identifying them," I said.

I went on to talk with Justin about preparing for his interviews. I pulled up a list on my phone, which I handed to him so he and Maya could give it a look. I suggested that Justin evaluate each applicant with these factors in mind:

⊃ **Team/Organization Cultural Fit**

Will the applicant agree and adhere to the expectations set for:

➡ Work schedules

➡ Team goals

➡ Professional integrity

➡ Business etiquette

⊃ **Current and Future Job-skill Capacity**

What is the applicant's ability to perform the duties of the position?

➡ Ability, aptitude, and necessary motivation to perform required functions

➡ Necessary credentials (if applicable)

⊃ **Interpersonal Skills**

Does the applicant have good communication and interaction skills?

➡ Caring, concern, and empathy for others

➡ Appropriate and effective listening skills

➡ Teamwork

➡ Flexibility

➡ Patience

➡ Dependability

⊃ **Past Performance and Accomplishments**

➡ Verifiable examples

"This is a great resource, Bogie," Justin said as he scrolled through while Maya looked over his shoulder.

"Thanks, man," I said. "Now, if you're bringing someone in at an entry-level position and they don't meet all of the criteria, they must have the ability and drive to grow into the job. But if you're hiring an applicant who has experience and is going to fill a senior role at the company, then they must possess the ability to contribute at an acceptable level shortly after coming on board."

"We're talking a lot about strengths, but what about weaknesses?" Maya asked.

"Good point," Justin added. "Shouldn't I be concentrating on an applicant's challenges as well as their abilities?"

I smiled, because I was just about to tell them a story about when I managed a team of instructional designers. We had a vacancy and I had set up a series of interviews with several candidates for the job. My initial screening of applicants involved reviewing their resumes and professional social media accounts. Once I evaluated the information, I chose the top five candidates whom I wanted to interview and scheduled them to come in and meet with me and the team.

One of the applicants, Tim Miller, clearly stood out. Tim arrived on time, was dressed appropriately, and seemed very well prepared. I met Tim in the lobby and exchanged introductions and pleasantries. I noticed that Tim struggled at maintaining eye contact and seemed somewhat anxious. Nothing was exceedingly out of the ordinary, but I just had a sense that Tim was a little more nervous than the other candidates. However, I wasn't too concerned. I know interviews are a stressful time and we all react differently.

We were doing panel interviews, so I brought Tim into the interview room and went through introductions with the team. I always start off my interviews with a friendly opening question, something along the lines of, "How was your commute? Any trouble finding the place?" It helps ease people into the process and relax.

Tim, nervously and with a little hesitation, responded that he had an easy commute and had no trouble finding our office since it was a short drive from his home. Then he forced a smile and said, "I guess it didn't hurt that I took five practice runs by the building over the last two days."

We all laughed and it relieved the tension in the room. We unanimously responded that at one time or another, we've all been there and did the same thing.

When the lighthearted discussion about the practice drive stopped and just as I was about to begin the formal interview, Tim looked at me and anxiously said, "I am not sure of the appropriate time or way to say this, but I have a form of social anxiety and I struggle with maintaining appropriate eye contact. Other people have said that when I am stressed or nervous, I come across as looking like I'm trying too hard to maintain eye contact. So, if that happens today, please know that I am not being rude or disrespectful."

I thanked Tim, told him that while it wasn't necessary to make that disclosure, I was glad that he did, because it really showed his courage. Then we went about the rest of the interview.

Maya and Justin were on the edge of their barstools as they listened to the story.

"Okay, I'm dying to know what happened!" she exclaimed.

"Did you offer him the job or not?" he asked.

"We did, and Tim accepted the position," I replied.

Maya pumped a fist in the air. "Yes! Go, Tim!"

Justin and I laughed.

"So was it a tough decision?" Justin wanted to know.

"Well, the pool of candidates were all extremely talented and capable, so yes, it was difficult to make a choice. The reason the panel decided to offer Tim the job was because the culture of the team was one of caring, inclusion, and honest communication. Tim displayed those exact traits by taking the risk to share with us a little about himself during the interview. That was over ten years ago and not only has Tim been a great asset to the team, but he has now advanced in the organization and manages the instructional design group."

"Wow, that's great," Maya said.

"It really is. And to this day, Tim's team continues to be recognized as a 'can do' group. The culture of valuing and promoting inclusion, honest communication, and high-performance achievement is solidly intact because of the hiring practices that have been established."

"That's the type of team that I want to be a part of," Justin replied.

"It didn't happen overnight, and it took me a while until we put the right policies and procedures in place to get the right people together," I said.

"You know, in my interviews, I haven't focused that much on the interpersonal skill set and how well of a fit the applicant would be with the team," he said, finally handing my phone back. "I always thought my interviewing technique was one of my strongest suits. Now, after talking it over with you, I see that I focused too much on the applicant's job experience and didn't put enough time into coming up with interview questions about team and culture fit." He let out a big sigh and said, "Looks like I have a lot of work in front of me when I get back." Then he quickly corrected himself, smiled and said, "No, a lot of *opportunity* in front of me."

I replied, "Justin, good for you. You have achieved a lot in a short period of time, and that is something to be proud of."

Then Maya chimed in. "Think about it. Your boss is here having dinner with you because you've made such a strong impression on him. You've proven that when we evolve, we breed success."

"Whoa, I love that saying!" I said.

Maya smiled. "You should tell my mom that. It's her mantra."

"I will," I said. "Speaking of which, maybe it's about time we rejoined her and David."

Maya looked at her watch. "Our orders should be up any minute now."

"Before we go back to the table, I want you to know that it was a pleasure getting to know you," I said. I couldn't believe it, but a lump was forming in my throat. "I want to wish you all the best. Please don't hesitate to check in from time to time."

Justin stopped me there. "Hold on a minute. This isn't goodbye. I was hoping that we could continue our discussions or coaching sessions remotely. Do you think that's possible?"

"Absolutely!" I said. "I'm eager to hear how you make out with your team when you get back."

We exchanged contact information and set up a remote meeting to catch up in two weeks.

Then Maya said, "I'll catch up with you both when I graduate, okay?" and we walked back over to our table where our food and guests were happily waiting.

Bogie's Notes

⊃ Be selective when adding new members to your team. Otherwise, you will pay for it later.

⊃ Interviews should go beyond experience. Think about company culture and a good fit for the team.

⊃ Let staff know that they're on your team because they've earned it.

chapter five

LVL Leadership IRL (In Real Life)

Acting on Team Feedback

"**B**ogie! It's great to see you," Justin said, smiling.

"You too, buddy. How's it going?"

Two weeks had passed since our last LVL dinner. Our first video chat was underway. I couldn't wait to hear how Justin was faring at work, given all we talked about while he was at the retreat.

"Pretty good," Justin said. "I haven't missed a day of exercise since we last met and I've dropped nine pounds. Honestly, I haven't felt this good in a long time."

"That's awesome, man," I said.

"I'm really looking forward to catching up. I have so much to tell you."

"Cool, let's dive in then."

Justin pulled out a notebook and began flipping through the pages. "Well, I feel like I'm accomplishing a great deal and starting to implement some of the things we discussed. But truthfully, I feel like I have more questions than answers about working with my team."

"Remember our discussion about loyalty on the night we first met?" I asked him.

"Not word for word, but generally, yes," he said.

"Okay, so in my line of work, when I meet with clients for the first time, they want one of two things from me," I explained. "To wave a magic wand and try to address years of issues in one conversation, or to show them how to go all-in with their employees and help them strengthen those relationships over time."

"So what happens when they want to take the short cut?" Justin asked while jotting something down in his notebook.

"To be honest, I'll respectfully decline to work with them, because it would be disingenuous," I responded.

"You really stick to your principles," he said.

"As a consultant, it can be hard to turn work away, but when you don't believe in the assignment or the objective, you have to," I said. "Anyway, I brought this up because it sounds like you have a lot more questions now because you and your team are communicating. And what that says to me is that you haven't given up on each other. You want to keep putting the time into your relationship because you value it, which I think is a great spot to be in, all things considered."

"That's a relief to hear," said Justin. "So how do we kick things off? I forgot to pick up some Yuengling."

I laughed. "Next time we can do a cyber happy hour. But for now, why don't we just start with one of your questions and go from there."

"Cool. So I've been thinking a lot about our conversations and I put together some steps in Personal and Organizational Improvement that I was hoping to share with my team when they're ready. Would you mind taking a look at them?" Justin asked.

"Would I mind?" I said with excitement. "Of course not!"

"Okay, I'm sending them to you now," Justin said.

I opened the email, clicked on the attachment, and read through Justin's steps, one by one.

Steps in Personal and Organizational Improvement

- **Stimuli or Exposure –** Individual is introduced to a new way of doing something, new technology, etc. "Better, quicker, faster, easier, more enjoyable, etc., way of doing something."

- **Call to Action** – Are you willing to take action? At The LVL, I could have opted to just talk and do nothing. Had I done nothing, odds are nothing would have improved and, more than likely, things would have stayed the same or may have gotten worse. However, I chose to act, and here we are today.

- **Education** – Increase your knowledge on the desired topic by discussing, reading, consulting with others, volunteering, etc.

- **Continuous Improvement** – It's a journey that doesn't end. Continue to review processes/actions for continuous improvement.

After reading through them, I had this feeling of pride come over me. I was really impressed that Justin put all of this together after our talks. He clearly was taking everything I said to heart, and that meant a lot.

"Justin, I think this list is amazing," I said. "It's totally spot-on."

His eyes lit up, like he was hoping I'd say that. "You really think so?"

"Absolutely," I said. "If you were here, I'd high five you."

He chuckled. "Thanks. I just can't believe where I am now, as opposed to two weeks ago. I'm hoping that I can replicate the same process with my staff."

"That's completely doable. It's just going to take some time," I said.

"As long as you're willing to stick with me, I've got plenty of time to spare," he replied.

I smiled. "Okay, hit me with your next question."

"Actually … I put together an agenda. I just sent it to you. Maybe we could go through it together?"

"Look at the initiative in Justin!" I said as I opened the file.

"I'm a new man, thanks to you," he said.

Agenda for Check-In with Bogie, February 18, 5:30 p.m.

⊃ **Self-Consistency**
- ➡ Physical
- ➡ Mental
- ➡ Spiritual

⊃ **Performance Management and Accountability**
- ➡ Individual (me) – Active Participation, Stay Positive, Volunteer
- ➡ Team
  - ⇨ Staff Departures – Any New Information
  - ⇨ Team Meeting – Discussion Topics
    - → Caring Environment
    - → Work/Life Balance
    - → Accountability
    - → Reward and Recognition

"No, thanks to YOU," I corrected him.

After reading through it, Justin started to talk about his overall health.

"Like I said, I've been exercising regularly and feel great about it. Also, I saw my primary care doctor and had my physical, which went well. He told me I was in good shape and was happy to hear I was running a bit. We even discussed the types of sneakers each of us had."

"I'm so glad to hear that," I said. "How are things going on the other fronts?"

"One thing that's really helped bring me more balance mentally is reading. I either read a magazine or a book at least 30 minutes each night before I go to bed," he said.

"That's great! Have you read anything you'd recommend?"

Justin thought for a moment and said, "I finished a book on management and leadership that's written by a CEO who used to be homeless. Super inspiring. And I'm halfway through a book on relationships my wife bought for me for Christmas last year."

"Both sound interesting," I said.

"They are. I've been lacking in both areas lately, and what I've learned in these two books alone has boosted my confidence because I feel so much more secure with all this new knowledge."

I nodded. "This might sound lame, but that is literally the power of reading. Every moment you spend opening your mind to new ideas is a moment well spent."

"That's not lame, it's just true."

"So what about spiritually?" I asked, feeling a little nervous. The last time I tried talking with Justin about this topic, things got awkward rather quickly. I didn't want that to happen again, of course, but I didn't want to avoid talking about it, either.

"Well, I'm still trying to define just exactly what that term means to me," Justin replied (thankfully without any hesitation). "For now, I feel like it's devoting myself to people and things that make me a better person."

"I like that," I said. "Could you give a few examples?"

"For one, I have started journaling every day. Nothing extensive, but first thing in the morning, I grab a cup of coffee and take a few minutes to write down what I am grateful for, significant things that are happening in my life, and what I want to get better at."

"Such as?"

"Let's see. Well, there are times when I just freeze up. Like if someone has a medical crisis in public. Other people are so quick to come and help, but usually I just stand there watching, unable to move."

I can tell by the way Justin's eyes drift off to the side that he feels vulnerable admitting this to me, so I quickly reassure him.

"Those situations are really tense, man. It's normal to panic a little."

Justin looked at me and grinned. "Thanks for saying that. The good news is, I wrote in my journal that I wanted to get past that fear somehow. And just this last weekend, something happened that put me to the test."

"Whoa, really?" I was definitely eager to hear his story, so I turned up the volume on my computer a notch or two.

"Yeah. I was at a local convenience store, standing in line waiting to pay for my purchase when a young gentleman behind me began to tremble. I wasn't sure what was happening, but in seconds, he crashed to the ground and had a seizure."

"That is super scary," I said.

"It was terrifying. Someone grabbed his arms and held them so he wouldn't hurt himself any further. I felt myself freezing up, but I took a deep breath and pushed through that feeling and helped out. I held down and immobilized his legs. Medical professionals arrived in a few minutes and took over. It appeared that the guy went into diabetic shock."

My thoughts immediately went to Maya's mom, Toni, and my heart ached a bit. I couldn't imagine how stressful living with diabetes could be.

"I know this type of thing isn't what we're here to discuss, but it was the first time I was able to spring into action like that, and it felt good helping someone else who was in trouble."

"Are you kidding? That's a huge accomplishment. I'm proud of you, Justin."

"Thanks, Bogie. I know spirituality is a tricky one for me and it will be an ongoing work in progress, but I do feel great about the direction I am heading."

"You should. And I think the journal is a great idea. You can really track your progress that way," I said. "Okay, what's next on the agenda?"

"Maybe we can talk about staff departures next?" he asked.

"Sure. Is there any new information?"

"Funny you should ask that," Justin said. "I actually called Colin, Aimee, and Jim to talk to them about why they left."

"Wow, that's bold," I said.

"Well, talking to you about possible reasons why they quit made me really curious," said Justin.

"I'm surprised that you reached out to Colin. Didn't you say you wouldn't rehire him because he didn't seem committed to the team?" I asked.

"That's precisely why I called him. I wanted to know if part of the reason Colin left was because of the way I was managing the team. Since he left to start his own business, I believed I'd have the best shot of getting an honest answer."

"Good point. So how'd it go?"

Justin sighed a little and then he chuckled, like he was remembering something funny about the conversation. "It took some time for Colin to trust me and open up as to why he left, but when he did, boy did he!"

"Uh oh," I said, wincing. "How bad was it? On a scale of one to ten?"

"Hmmmm … maybe an eleven."

"Ouch."

"Yeah. Colin started off by saying he'd always wanted to start his own business, but he hadn't planned on doing it for another three or more years," Justin explained. "Colin also said that he believed the team was in trouble because of me. He was concerned that I seemed on the outs with senior leadership and that I was no longer leading but rather just keeping us on autopilot."

As I listened to Justin say all of these negative things about himself, I couldn't help but notice that he didn't seem discouraged or act like his feelings had been hurt. In fact, Justin seemed very composed, like all of this feedback was something he needed to hear, even though it must have been difficult.

Justin continued, "Colin said he was concerned I was becoming less and less engaged with the team. He even went on to say that he was worried about my health, too. Basically, everything we discussed on the first night we met, Colin noticed. He said that he was glad I called and that I seemed to be in a better place."

"That was nice of him," I said.

"You're right. Frankly, his honesty, even though it bordered on brutal sometimes, was a true gift. It was just the validation I needed to keep me on this path. And the conversation gave me the opportunity to apologize for not being the leader he deserved. I could tell he appreciated that."

"I'm sure he did. Holding yourself accountable must have been hard, but it's the only way to keep people's faith in you."

"Well said, Bogie. As I left Colin's office and got in my car, it really hit me. My best employees left *me*, not the company. It was painful to admit, but the good news is I'm doing something to change that."

I smiled. "You sure are. So what happened with Aimee and Jim?"

"I'm having lunch with Aimee next week and I left a message for Jim. He hasn't returned my call yet, but hopefully we'll connect," he said.

Justin and I spent a few minutes prepping for his lunch meeting with Aimee, such as what he would like to discuss, as well as what she may want to talk about. Justin said he planned on starting the conversation by thanking her for agreeing to see him, letting her know about the changes he was making, and apologizing if he was the reason she left. It sounded like a solid plan.

Then we moved on to the Team Meeting topic. Justin mentioned that he held a team meeting last week to discuss the topics and information presented at the senior leadership conference. Justin also shared with his staff some of the personal changes he was working on incorporating into his life, both personally and professionally. In addition to the agenda that had been prepared for the team, Justin stressed the point that he wanted to do a better job of improving his communication with the group and encouraged his staff to ask all the questions they wanted.

"I explained to the team how I realized I'd been underperforming in that area and asked for their feedback as I work to improve with sharing information," he said.

"How'd they react?" I asked.

"They seemed skeptical, but as I shared my notes from the senior leadership retreat, people started commenting on how this was the first time they'd ever heard anything that came out of those meetings," he replied. "I also told my boss, David, that the staff seemed to appreciate the information I shared with them. David actually thanked me for letting him know and asked if I would take the lead in ensuring that the organization did a better job disseminating information to the staff."

"That's awesome, Justin. He seems to really believe in you," I said.

Justin smiled. "It definitely feels good to have him in my corner."

"You know, I really ought to commend you on your openness and willingness to share some of your personal and professional challenges with your team. As we've discussed before, transparency is key," I said. "But I just want to remind you there is a fine line between disclosing too little and too much."

Justin jotted something down in his notebook and said, "Keep talking."

"Well, it's been my experience that when leaders make a new commitment to improve communication and openness, at times they go overboard and share too much. There are certain topics that exceed professional boundaries and are not to be disclosed."

"I know this seems like common sense, but I'm going to ask for an example, just to be on the safe side," Justin said.

"Okay, here's an example. I once worked with a client who was trying to create more open lines of communication between him and his staff. He was making real progress, but then he started considering himself more of a peer than a leader."

Justin scratched his head. "And that's bad because…?"

"He started to lose his authority. And not the bad kind of authority that insecure managers often use to intimidate everyone…"

"The good kind you need to successfully lead," finished Justin.

"Exactly," I said. "As you and your staff begin to feel more comfortable talking with each other, you'll be tempted to share more and more. Just remember to take time to think about what you want to say and how you are going to say it."

"Should we put together a list or something?" he suggested. "Those have been helping me stay on track."

"Absolutely," I said.

After a few minutes of brainstorming, we wrote down the following:

Great topics to share

➡ Information that strengthens the team and helps to build trust

➡ Timely (and disclosable) information about changes in the organization or the work unit

➡ Team accomplishments or successes

➡ "Been there" moments – opportunities to bond with the team by sharing lessons learned from some of your own obstacles, ones you've experienced that the team may be going through

Topics not to be shared (let your conscience guide you):

➡ Anything you wouldn't say in the presence of others

➡ Medical or HR issues

➡ Information told to you in confidence

➡ Organizational information that is not public yet

Once we had completed the list, I said, "Remember, Justin. You can never let your guard down as a leader. Your team is always watching and listening to all you do and say. A leader sets the tone of what is acceptable and not acceptable."

"I won't forget, Bogie," he said, smiling.

"So how did the rest of your meeting go?" I asked.

"Couldn't have gone any better. I wound up asking the team to write down the areas that could use the most improvement, along with what kinds of changes they'd like to see, both with the team culture and with my leadership," he said. "Then I left the room so they could have privacy. The team charted their comments on flipchart paper. Here, I'll send you some pictures. It's so weird how their notes mirrored everything we discussed at The LVL."

WHAT A CARING WORK ENVIRONMENT MEANS TO US

Take action or explain why you can't.

✔ **Follow through with commitments**

   ✗ Example: Assignment of additional work with the promise of more staff. Yet, additional staff never comes ... UGH!

✔ **Recognize our time and our workloads**

   ✗ Example: All-employee mandatory lunches are scheduled at such times that they often interfere with work deadlines. If we go to the luncheon, we must work late to ensure deadlines are met. It's as if we're being penalized for attending a work event. CHANGE THIS!

✔ **Be our advocate**

   ✗ Example: Sales invoices are posting incorrectly to the commission compensation software. We have identified the issues and have a solution, but the information technology department has us at the bottom of their "to do" list. This adds eight additional hours of work per month for what can be an "easy fix." HELP!

WHAT WORK/LIFE BALANCE MEANS TO US

Let us have the opportunity to thrive at work and at home.

✔ Scheduling Flexibility
  ✗ When possible, allow us to manage our time so that we can attend life events (school functions for the kids, eldercare appointments, etc.) and still accomplish our workload.

✔ Independence
  ✗ Determine what work assignments can be done remotely and consider allowing us to telecommute more.

✔ Consistency
  ✗ Get management on the same page. Some branches, identical to ours, are allowed greater work flexibilities than we are. Why?

WHAT ACCOUNTABILITY MEANS TO US

Management creates an environment where we are given the equipment and resources to achieve optimal performance and then holds us to a defined standard for achieving it.

✔ Stop "punishing" high-performers
  ✗ Please hold everyone accountable. It seems the better an employee you are, the more work you get. On the other hand, the more difficult someone is to work with, it's as if they get rewarded by being left alone and not given any additional work.

✔ Be clear
  ✗ Be clear with expectations and how we will be held accountable. While it doesn't happen often, it hurts when we think we're doing a good job only to find out that the final product isn't what you expected. We care and want to do a good job but feel horrible when we let you down. Please be clear on your expectations.

HOW WE WANT TO BE
REWARDED AND RECOGNIZED

Rewards and recognition should be earned, celebrated,
and given in a timely manner.

NOTE: Please know we are grateful for any reward or recognition
and appreciate it. With that said, as requested, below are some
thoughts the team came up with on the topic. (Thank you for
asking. 😄)

✔ Individual recognition
  ✗ For individual awards, ask us how we'd like to be rewarded
    (when possible). Some of us would prefer time off over
    financial rewards and others vice-versa.

✔ Group Recognition
  ✗ Let's celebrate more team accomplishments or milestones.
    We don't have that much time to come together as a group,
    but even a 10-minute gathering with some refreshments
    would be nice.

✔ More "Peer Award Recognition"
  ✗ We would love to have a process where we could nominate
    each other for smaller awards or recognition.

P.S. Thank you for asking us about our thoughts on these topics.
We really appreciate it! This was a great exercise!!!

After looking at the pictures, I was kind of floored by how engaged Justin's team was. He was a lucky manager.

"Wow, this feedback is invaluable. It's amazing that your staff really rose to the occasion here," I said.

"I know. They're a great group," Justin said. "And I'm committed to meeting their needs as their leader. I promised I'd get back to them before the end of the month to discuss their suggestions and let them know what I would and wouldn't be able to implement."

"Awesome stuff," I said.

"I'm also starting the recruitment process so I can replace Colin, Aimee, and Jim. It won't be easy, but it has to get done," he said.

"You're right."

I looked at the clock on my screen and noticed we were running out of time, so we began to wrap things up. Once we had a quick review of his most recent accomplishments, we started planning our next video chat in two months. Together, Justin and I came up with a list of things to do until we spoke again.

1. **Celebrate victories!** Remember to take time to acknowledge successes and share them with friends and family.

2. **Review staff's list of suggestions again.** Implement whatever is possible immediately and let them know what's being done behind the scenes. For example, let them know of efforts to provide them more support with the other division directors. A leader's job is to remove obstacles that are getting in the way of their team's success.

3. **Continue to journal and manage time** like the precious commodity it is.

4. **Take detailed notes** on the meeting with Aimee and conversation with Jim (if he ever responds).

I wasn't expecting to hear from Justin until our next scheduled call, but two weeks later, Justin texted and asked if I had a few minutes. Apparently he was running into some personal challenges. Naturally I was a bit concerned, so we hopped on the phone right away.

"Everything okay, Justin?" I asked.

"Mostly." His voice sounded a little softer than usual. "The team is doing well, and work is coming together, but I'm having a hard time staying focused on my own goals and commitments that I set for myself."

Justin explained that he hadn't exercised for a week and he even stopped journaling. Basically, everything had been going so well, but now he felt like he'd "hit a wall" and just wasn't able to find the motivation that had been fueling him the last month.

"Sorry to bother you with all this," Justin said, sounding very defeated.

"Are you kidding? I'm happy you reached out," I said. "Listen, self-improvement and development is a journey, and no one ever said it was going to be easy."

"I guess I just didn't expect it to be so exhausting."

"Hey, mind if I tell you a story?" I asked.

Justin chuckled a little. "Honestly, I was hoping you would."

With Justin's blessing, I launched into a story about a lunch I had with my long-time friend Gary, who worked in human resources. Gary was always impeccably dressed, and although he was in his seventies, no one would have ever guessed it. He appeared to be at least twenty years younger.

I'd asked Gary how he was able to take such great care of himself.

He laughed and told me, "Bogie, you don't think for one second that I don't want the extra dessert, hamburger, or beer. Or sleep in and not go to the gym?"

Gary had said every day was a little struggle. But after stumbling and falling repeatedly, he realized that the only way to feel as healthy as he wanted was to eat well and in moderation, as well as follow his exercise regime. To this day, he still relapses. Some weeks were easier than others and some were worse than others, but he made a promise to himself that he'd never give up.

"So, Justin, at that moment it dawned on me. Gary was no different than I am. His health doesn't come naturally to him, and he has to work at it," I explained. "He was just more disciplined. Quitting was never an option for him. And, when he fell off the wagon, he didn't overanalyze it. He just got back to what he was supposed to be doing."

"Gary sounds like a pretty cool guy," Justin replied.

"He is, but we're all the same, man. The only thing that differentiates us is how fast we recover and get back on the horse," I said.

"I guess you're right." Justin's voice sounded stronger, which definitely made me sigh with relief.

"What else do you have planned for the day?" I asked.

"I'm going to leave the office in a few minutes and head home for dinner."

"Do you think you have enough time to journal before you head out?"

"I think so."

"Okay, great. As soon as we end this call, write an entry in your journal," I suggested. "Then, when you get home, have a sensible dinner. Maybe after that, you could go for a walk with your family."

Justin laughed and said, "Just like that, I guess I'm back on track?"

"Almost. Yup, just like that."

"What's the 'almost' about?"

"The 'almost' is made up of two conditions. The first is that you journal, make smart food choices, and get your exercise in. The second condition, which I believe is equally as important as the first, is that you can't ever beat yourself up over stumbling. Falling down is how we learn. Just keep your eyes on the road ahead of you, not behind you."

"Thanks, man. I really appreciate the pep talk," Justin said.

"That's what friends are for."

Bogie's Notes

➲ Don't be afraid to share with your staff, but know where to draw the line.

➲ It's okay to bond with your direct reports, but leaders must remain authority figures, not peer-level buddies.

➲ Your shared journey to self-improvement and development is just that … a journey. Expect bumps in the road and detours, but also be sure to take time to celebrate the victories.

chapter six

Team Synergy

Everyone Contributes

Six weeks later, Justin and I were video chatting again. This time we both remembered to bring a bottle of Yuengling to our meeting. After making a toast, we jumped right in to the work at hand.

"Not the same as draft, but still damn good," Justin said.

"You took the words right out of my mouth!"

"Bogie, I appreciate that call we had a few weeks ago. You really helped me out," he said.

I smiled. "No problem. I'm always around if you need a hand."

"Thanks."

"So what's happening at work? How's the team doing?" I asked.

"Pretty good," Justin replied. "We had another meeting and I told the group that I reviewed their suggestions and made two lists. The first list was easy because it contained all the changes that I would carry out immediately. The second list was made up of items that I needed to spend more time on or get additional information before I could tackle them."

"Sounds like a great approach," I said.

Justin went on. "One of the areas that I was most concerned about was the fact that we are understaffed. I knew that hiring a professional at a senior level wasn't something that I could resolve in the next sixty days. So I asked the team what I could do to help alleviate some of the pressure. We had an awesome discussion and we all came to the consensus that bringing on support staff as soon as possible would be a good solution."

"That's so cool. You were all able to come up with a solution together," I said.

"I know, it was awesome to troubleshoot with each other. Gwen, who is usually reserved and isn't really that vocal in staff meetings, suggested we make inclusivity a priority. Everyone loved that idea and she offered to contact the county's Office of Vocational Rehabilitation and see if they may have someone who might be interested in the job."

"It must have been amazing to see someone like Gwen getting more involved," I said.

"It was so awesome to see her take initiative. I even asked Gwen if she wouldn't mind coordinating everything with human resources. She beamed from ear to ear. She was really happy to be taking on a new role."

"So what happened? Did you wind up hiring anyone?"

"We did," Justin said with excitement. "His name is Karl. He is on the autism spectrum, so we set him up with a job coach for a couple of days to learn about his duties. He caught on super fast, and with his help, I could see everyone breathing a little easier since they had the additional support."

"That's fantastic," I said.

"Yeah, hiring Karl has definitely helped boost morale, and everyone just seems happier," Justin said, grinning. "Oh, and Gwen stopped by my office the other day to thank me for listening to her idea and empowering her to run with it. Apparently she has a sister who has benefited from the same Office of Vocational Rehabilitation and she was grateful to be able to pay it forward and let someone else feel the joy that her family has felt ever since her sister found a job she loved."

"Wow, that had to feel good," I said.

"Bogie, I have to tell you, that interaction gave me such a rush. Gwen also told me the team has been saying things have changed for the better ever since I came back from the retreat. She said communication has improved, I'm acting on their suggestions when I'm able to, and letting them know why I can't or won't when I'm not able to. Gwen also agreed that there seems to be a better vibe in the office, and she said, '*Whatever you're doing, keep it up. It's working, and we appreciate it.*'"

"Justin, you do realize why Gwen said those things, don't you?" I asked, then instantly answered my own question. "It's because it's true. You are listening, empowering your team, acting on the things you can do something about, and giving honest feedback about the things you can't. Earning the respect and loyalty of your staff was a big priority and you're achieving that."

Justin laughed under his breath and took another sip of beer. "Well, don't get too excited. I had lunch with Aimee and it was very humbling."

"Okay, well, what was the overall takeaway?"

"Basically, Aimee didn't want to leave the organization, but she left because of me. She said she didn't think the team was going to make it and that she was fearful of being let go because we weren't performing well."

I cringed a little. "That must have hurt to hear."

Justin shrugged. "It did, but I tried to see it as an opportunity to be accountable, so I apologized to Aimee and told her that I felt horrible for letting her down. I explained that I was going through a rough time at work and just wasn't aware of how it was affecting the people on my team. Anyway, Aimee mentioned that she keeps in touch with people from the office, and although she was a little frustrated that things had gotten better after she left, she was glad that things were improving, for everyone else's sake."

"That was good of her to say."

"Yeah, I mean, I don't blame her for feeling frustrated. Given the circumstances, I could see why anyone would feel that way."

"How's her new job going?" I asked.

"Apparently very well. But it's new to her, so she's still navigating her way around the organization and learning who is who and what is what. You know, I asked her if she would ever consider coming back and give me a second chance," Justin said.

"You did?" I said with surprise.

"Well, I figured I didn't have anything to lose!"

"True," I said. "What did she say?"

"She asked me how long I could give her to decide. I told her that I made a commitment to the team to fill her position as soon as possible, but given she knows the job and we wouldn't have to retrain her, I could give her a month to think it over."

"That seems totally fair," I said.

"She thought so, too," he said. "I'm going to keep interviewing, of course, but I hope she seriously considers it."

"Any word from Jim?" I asked.

"Nope. Nothing."

"That's okay. It's good that you tried to reconnect, but ultimately everyone calls their own shots and Jim must have his reasons for not responding. You need to continue to focus your energy on where you can make an impact."

"I feel the same way," Justin said. "The other thing I wanted to tell you is that things with David, my boss, are getting better every day."

"Really? That's great," I said.

"I'm chairing a committee for improving communication throughout the company and it's been a wonderful experience. We've installed sharing boards, which are nothing more than dry-erase boards, in each division to make it easier for employees to swap information with each other."

"Nice. How did everyone respond to them?"

"Great. We just put them up and invited staff to post anything on them that would be beneficial for others to know," Justin replied. "We've had people post birthday announcements, requests for assistance with various projects, and even words of encouragement or congratulations to co-workers. It's amazing how something so simple has had such a huge impact throughout the organization."

"This is exciting stuff," I said. "What about everything at home? Any updates there?"

"Believe it or not, my wife and I are now going to the gym together," Justin said. "It's been a nice bonding experience for us and we're feeling better – and closer – than we have in years!"

"That's music to my ears, man," I said.

Soon our time was up, so Justin and I agreed to meet again in two months and set the following agenda for our next meeting:

➡ **Hiring**

⇨ Continue recruiting additional staff, but under no circumstances should hiring be done with a "close enough" mentality. Managers need to ensure that new staff will be the right fit.

➡ **Delegation/Mentoring**

⇨ Hand off projects that are energy killers and focus on being available to lead the team, running "interference" for them, etc. Also, think about the team members with leadership potential and what could be done to develop them.

➡ **Career Development/Progression**

⇨ Start thinking about future goals and what a happy, fulfilling life looks like. Also, look into retirement savings and other things that will be a part of "the next chapter."

The last item seemed to make Justin a bit overwhelmed.

"I haven't given much thought to the future or retirement," he said. "For once, I feel good about myself, my family, and my work. I just want to enjoy the present."

"I understand. Being in the present and enjoying life is extremely important. However, time is a continuum and doesn't stop for anyone. The future eventually becomes the present and we need to prepare for it."

Bogie's Notes

⊃ Earn your staff's loyalty and respect by listening to and empowering them.

⊃ If staff needs something to be done, do it. If that's not possible, be honest by letting them know, and why.

chapter seven

The Role of Delegation

Developing Future Leaders

Two months later, Justin and I were having another after-work video meeting, fresh bottles of Yuengling in hand. I couldn't help but notice that Justin looked leaner than he had the last time we talked, and he'd even gotten a new haircut. He easily looked ten years younger and was radiating confidence. It was so exciting to see.

"So how's recruitment going, Justin? Any new hires?"

Justin smiled. "Yes, actually. We filled one of our vacancies and we couldn't have gotten a better hire."

"Cool, I'd love to hear about them," I said.

"Well, you already have," he said, laughing. "It's Aimee."

"Whoa! You're kidding!"

"I'm totally serious," Justin said. "About a week after we met, Aimee called and asked if we could discuss the job opportunity again. Long story short, Aimee said that she spoke with some people at the office to see if things were truly improving and everyone she talked to went to bat for the team and confirmed that things have really changed."

"That's awesome," I said.

"Anyway, Aimee's back onboard and picked up right where she left off. She said she felt bad about leaving the other organization she was with, but she knew coming back was the right move and the better fit."

"That's great news. I'm so happy for you both."

"Thanks," Justin said.

"So how about the other open positions? Has there been any progress?" I asked.

"Sort of. I never forgot our discussion about ensuring that we make the absolute best hire possible and to never settle for less, but high standards are not easy to meet," Justin replied. "I teamed up with someone in HR and we reviewed hundreds of resumes and interviewed over twenty-five candidates over the past couple of months. When I thought I found an ideal candidate, the team members on the panel didn't agree with me, and when they found what they believed to be an ideal candidate, I didn't agree."

"Yeah, it can feel like gridlock when that happens," I said.

"True. But I've stayed positive and took comfort in the fact that the team was just as adamant about finding the best candidate as I was. Gwen was the first panel member to point out that making the right selection was going to take time and we had to be patient. She said, and I quote, '*Our team is in such a great place and we need to preserve that by being meticulous about vetting our new hire.*'"

I smiled. "I gotta say, I don't know Gwen at all, but somehow she's my favorite person ever."

"Cheers to Gwen," Justin said, raising his beer. "Anyway, because we were having such a difficult time trying to hire another person at the journeyman level, I recommended that we hire someone at an entry-level trainee position instead."

"Oh, good idea," I said.

"The team seemed to think so, too. HR announced the job for a management analyst in our instructional design division on the company's website and some other recruiting sites. I haven't told anyone this, but I called our good friend Maya from The LVL and asked if she would be interested in applying."

Naturally, I couldn't contain my excitement. "No way! How is Maya? What did she say? Did she send in an application?"

I rattled off these questions so fast, Justin nearly spit out his beer with laughter.

"Slow down, Bogie," he said, chuckling.

"Sorry, sorry. I just love the idea of Maya working for your company. She has so much potential and you could be a great mentor to her," I explained.

Justin grinned. "Thanks for saying that. It means a lot coming from you."

"Did you find out how Maya's mom is?" I asked.

"She's made a full recovery," Justin said with a sigh of relief.

"That's fantastic," I said. "And what happened with Maya? Was she interested in the job?"

"She was really excited to hear about the opportunity," he said. "She was finishing up her last business class, so she applied and HR immediately called her in for an interview without knowing I had any involvement whatsoever."

"That's a really good sign," I said.

"You should have seen Maya at the interview," Justin said, smiling as he thought back to that moment. "She was so poised and confident. She had everyone eating out of the palm of her hand."

"Well, that doesn't surprise me one bit."

"You know, it was clear as day she'd studied all the notes from our sessions at The LVL. I counted a few Bogie-isms in her answers, and of course, the panel just loved them," Justin said.

"Really? Aw, I'm so flattered that she took my words to heart," I said.

"Of course she did. They're great words," Justin replied. "Anyway, we interviewed seven candidates for the position and Maya was the team's No. 1 pick!"

"That's amazing," I said.

"Maya was super excited to get the offer and she accepted – after negotiating her starting salary a bit," Justin said.

"That young lady has such a good head on her shoulders," I said.

"Definitely," he said. "She starts in two weeks. We're really lucky to have her."

"So I have to ask – did you ever mention that you knew Maya before she came into interview?"

I was worried about asking this question because I didn't want to rain on Justin's parade, but I felt like we needed to discuss how personal relationships can color someone's judgment a bit, especially when it comes to hiring a new team member.

"I haven't said anything yet," Justin replied.

"Any idea why not?"

Justin took a beat or two and then admitted, "I didn't want anyone to think I was biased, I guess. I wanted the panel to give Maya the benefit of the doubt and for Maya to succeed on her own merits, not because of my influence."

"That all makes perfect sense," I said. "I just want to point out that being transparent with your colleagues is very important. What if Maya says something to a co-worker about knowing you from the retreat, or your boss, Mr. Robinson, makes a comment to someone about the dinner we shared. What do you think your staff will think of you?"

"Probably that I can't be fully trusted," Justin said, his face crumpling a bit. "Did I just make a huge mistake?"

"It's not a problem that can't be fixed," I reassured him. "Maybe before Maya's start date you could explain to the panel that you referred her to the job but kept that information to yourself so she could have a fair shot during the interview. I'm sure they'll understand and feel good that they're hearing it from you first. Besides, they all seemed to like her independently, so there's no harm done."

Justin jotted down some notes and nodded along. "Great advice. Thanks, Bogie."

"No problem," I said. "So what's next on the agenda? Oh yeah, developing your staff by delegating more and more ownership, responsibility, and assignments to them."

By the way his shoulders began to sag, I could see that Justin's confidence was wilting a bit.

"Well, I'm not going to lie. It's been a struggle. It seems like it takes a lot longer to show them how to complete a project than just doing it myself, which I end up doing because I want to save time," he said.

"I hear you. Delegation is one of the most challenging things for managers to conquer," I said. "But here's the thing – if you continue to do everything yourself, you're cheating your staff out of teachable moments and the opportunity to develop. Also, you might save some time in the short term, but eventually it robs you of time that can be spent doing important work, like improving operations, growing the business, and even being with your family."

"You're making a lot of good points," Justin said as he continued to take notes.

"Here's something else to consider," I continued. "What happens in the event you suddenly aren't there? Who is going to do the work? I know, I know, the work will get done because it always does. But think how much easier it would be on staff if they have completed projects before versus having second- or third-hand knowledge of how they are done."

"That's true. In an emergency situation, my team would have to overcome more obstacles because they don't have as much hands-on experience," he replied.

"Okay, here's the last thing I want to say. Delegating projects allows you to evaluate a staff member's leadership potential," I said. "Justin, don't think for one second that you aren't being evaluated, too. Remember, someone is always watching, and when your leadership team observes you performing assignments that your staff should be doing, what do you think they are thinking?"

After a brief pause, which seemed like an eternity, Justin responded, "Bogie, you got me again. I know how important delegation is and I keep meaning to delegate more projects. It's just that things are going so well right now. The team is really clicking, and I'm worried that if I put more on their plates, it's going to hurt their morale."

I nodded and said, "I understand your concern, but can you tell me how many days a week you are staying late to finish your work?"

Justin replied, "Three or four. But we're still understaffed, and I can't expect my direct reports to stay late all the time."

"You're right, you can't expect that. But staying and working late should be the exception and not the norm, even for managers. Before you know it, you're going to burn out and you'll end up right where you started. Eventually, everyone will be back to square one. Your staff will become resentful again because they won't be given opportunities and productivity will go down. What happens next?"

Justin rubbed his temples and then blew out a sigh. "My staff will quietly suffer and disengage. Some might work extra hard to make it better and weather the storm until something gives. And some will just leave."

"Wasn't that what one of our first discussions was about?" I asked.

Justin nodded. "Yes. I'm embarrassed to admit it, but I was giving up on myself back then. I didn't feel like I had any control over what happened at my job."

"But we both know that you do," I said. "I know it's hard to not fall back into old patterns because they're familiar. But if we don't learn from the past –"

"We're doomed to repeat it," Justin chimed in.

"Unfortunately, it's true," I said.

Justin smiled, looked at me, and said with a laugh, "Well, I'm not about to backslide, and I don't think you'd ever let that happen, Bogie!"

I laughed and replied, "You're right, I wouldn't! But seriously, Justin, you're the one doing all the hard work. I really admire how committed you are. I can't tell you how many clients I work with who love to talk a big game when it comes to leadership, but they aren't willing to roll up their sleeves and do what needs to be done."

"I promise, I'm not one of those people," Justin said.

"You don't need to promise. I knew that about you after one dinner," I said, smiling.

As we ended our session, Justin agreed to focus on delegating assignments and we set a date to meet again in three months. But there was a surprise in store for me that I didn't see coming, and boy, did it throw me for a curve.

Bogie's Notes

⊃ It may be easier to do things yourself, but that shortchanges staff's teachable moments and opportunities to improve.

⊃ Delegating not only says "I believe in you," but it also frees up time to focus on bigger matters, not only at work but at home.

⊃ When you delegate, you give someone else the spotlight to show his or her leadership potential.

chapter eight

The Boss Is On Line 1

Honoring Confidentiality

A few days after my last video call with Justin, I heard from David Robinson, Justin's boss. He called and wanted to discuss retaining my firm's services, which honestly I had forgotten about given how busy I was with work and my sessions with Justin.

"I'm really sorry it's taken me so long to get back in touch," David said.

"No worries. I know how hectic things can be at the office," I replied.

"I was hoping that you might be available to present and facilitate a series of management and leadership development courses. We think they could be extremely helpful for our employees," he said.

"That's great. I'd love to be involved."

"What about individual executive coaching sessions for the managers and leaders? Is that something else we could add into the mix?" he asked.

"Sure, we offer those services, too. No problem," I said.

As we wrapped up the details, David asked me if I had a few moments to discuss a challenge he was working through.

"Now that I'm a client, I'm hoping that this conversation will be confidential," he said.

"Of course. What did you want to talk about?"

"Well, I'm sure you're not surprised to hear that our management team is very impressed with Justin's leadership. Even though his team continues to be understaffed, their performance has improved so much. They've already accomplished many of their year-end goals," David said.

"That's incredible. I'm so happy for everyone," I said.

David continued, "So the executive committee is thinking about promoting Justin into an executive vice president role."

I almost combusted when those words left his mouth. JUSTIN MIGHT GET PROMOTED! But I remained calm and said to David, "Justin has made huge strides and I think he would be a great choice for that position."

"There is one reservation everyone has, though," David hedged, his voice sounding skeptical.

My heart felt like it was dropping into my stomach. This was such a pivotal moment in Justin's career and it seemed like everything was going to hinge on my conversation with David. *"How did I get into this situation?"* I thought to myself. But then my brain responded, *"Because you're Bogie, that's why!"*

Who am I to argue with my own brain?

After what seemed like a gigantic awkward pause, I asked, "Okay, what's the one reservation?"

"All of the execs have noticed that Justin is staying later and later. He's also still attending meetings that his staff should assume responsibility for," he explained. "Naturally, there are some concerns about Justin's ability to develop his staff in a way that's going to pay off for the company in the long term. What do you think? Would you agree?"

My breath caught in my throat as I tried to think of the right way to answer his question. I obviously wasn't going to betray Justin's confidence and tell David anything Justin and I had discussed in our sessions. But at the same time, I couldn't deny how it appeared David was shirking his responsibilities as a leader by asking someone else to tip the scales in this tough decision. I didn't want to offend David by pointing that out, but I felt like I owed it to Justin to help David make this assessment on his own.

So I swallowed hard and spoke up.

"I'm not sure it's important what I think, because ultimately you and your colleagues have seen what Justin can do firsthand," I said.

There was a silence on the end of the line. I got nervous waiting for David to say something, so I just kept talking.

"I'm sure that Justin has areas in which he can improve. Nobody's perfect. But maybe there's a way you can help him fine-tune his performance," I said.

"How?" was David's short reply. I couldn't quite read his tone, and I hoped I wasn't overstepping.

"Well, you could be transparent about the situation. You could tell Justin that he has what it takes to advance, but that you feel like he'll need to hone his delegation skills first," I suggested. "You don't have to make any promises, of course. But your feedback could be the difference between Justin getting the promotion or being overlooked."

David was quiet again. After a beat or two, he said, "That's good advice. I'm meeting with him next month. I could talk with him about it then."

While I was relieved that David seemed open to my thoughts, waiting for a month to bring the matter up with Justin kind of went against the founding tenants of LVL Leadership. The sooner you can talk about issues, the better!

So I went out on another limb.

"It's great that you already have a meeting set up, but if you and the committee believe this is the only thing that needs to be resolved before you can promote Justin, would there be any harm in meeting him this week?"

"Why does it matter?" David asked.

"Well, think of it this way. The sooner you tell Justin what skills he should work on, the quicker he can improve, rise through the ranks, and make a bigger impact on the company," I said.

Thankfully, there wasn't a long silence after that statement.

"I think you're right," David said. "I may have been putting the conversation off because Justin has really turned things around and I didn't want him to feel like I wasn't appreciative of everything he's done. I can tell he cares deeply about others and doing the best job he can. I don't want to discourage him."

"That makes a lot of sense. But look at it this way, you can also make that meeting an opportunity to tell Justin all the things he's doing well and praise him for it. Once he knows you value his work, he'll be eager to hear what else he can do to grow at the company."

"Fair enough. I'll reschedule the meeting for next week," he decided.

As we wrapped up the conversation, David said, "Bogie, thanks for taking Justin under your wing. Oh, and I ran into Maya in the hall the other day and I wasn't sure who was happier to see whom: me or her!"

I wiped some sweat off my forehead, sighing in relief that I hadn't taken any missteps with David. "Say 'hi' to Maya for me! And congratulations!"

"I will," he said. "Take care, Bogie. We'll be in touch."

Bogie's Notes

⟳ Your workers' trust is essential. Keeping their confidence is a must.

⟳ When possible, coach others to come up with solutions themselves.

chapter nine

Move Over, Move Up, or Move On

Pushing the Ball Forward

"I can't believe this is our last video call. What am I going to do without you?" Justin said sadly as he nursed his beer.

"You're going to do fine. Trust me," I said, trying not to sound as sad as he did, but failing miserably.

Three months had flown by, and in that time, I'd emailed Justin to tell him that I thought our next mentoring session should be our last. It was a hard letter for me to write because I really enjoyed talking with Justin. But at the same time, I kept feeling like we both needed to spread our wings a bit. Justin had learned so much, and I was sure the moment he got promoted, he'd be extremely busy adapting to the new role. As for me, I wanted to throw myself into a new project, but that was as far as my thoughts would take me.

"I do trust you, Bogie. But that doesn't mean I'm not going to miss talking with you," Justin said.

"It's not like we're never going to talk again. My lecture series starts next month and I expect you to be in the front row at all of them," I replied.

"Yes, sir," Justin said, saluting me jokingly.

I laughed. "So what's the good word at the office?"

"Well, a couple months ago, I had a great performance planning session with David. Get this – I'm being considered for a promotion to an executive vice president position!"

My mouth widened with pretend shock. "Are you kidding me? That's fantastic. Congrats, man! You deserve it."

Justin rolled his eyes. "Bogie, come on. You already knew, right?"

"Is my acting that bad?" I said, chuckling.

"I just figured that you two had talked, since he mentioned he hired you to come in to do executive coaching and everything," he explained. "Bogie, I have to ask, and not that it matters – but did you discuss our last call with him, because the similarities between what he was saying and our conversation was scary!"

My pulse started to race at the thought of Justin feeling like his privacy had been breached, so I quickly tried to reassure him. "Full disclosure – David did ask for my input on your performance, but I didn't tell him anything you and I had discussed. Actually, I suggested he come to you with his concerns."

"And I'm so glad you did," Justin said, to my relief. "My meeting with David went really well. He was open with me in a way that he'd never been, and because you and I had our discussion about delegation the week before, I'd put together a list of duties that I wanted to hand off to my team."

"Oh, cool! You were prepared then," I said.

"I was more than prepared. By the time I talked with David, I'd already met with my staff and delegated a bunch of projects. David was taken aback when he realized I was already working on the changes. He said he was extremely pleased with my overall performance. It felt so good to hear."

"You should be proud of yourself, Justin. That promotion is yours, I know it," I said.

We spent some more time wrapping up a few other topics, and then it came time to say our farewells. We both knew we'd be seeing each other again soon, but somehow the finality of this last LVL Leadership session was making me choke up a little. I could see Justin was feeling that way, too.

Still, that didn't change that our time together was over.

"So, I'm wondering do you remember the one condition I had when I first offered you my help at The LVL?" I asked him.

Justin paused, reflected, and then smiled. "Yes. You simply asked that I pay it forward and help someone else."

I smiled back. "That's right! And now, Justin, it's your turn. You have accomplished so much, and you have so much to offer.

There are a lot of folks who need a leg up and someone to give them a boost. You have worked so hard to achieve everything you have now, and you're strong enough to lace your fingers together and give someone that much-needed boost. Do you still think that's something you're willing to do?"

Justin raised his beer and said, "I do so solemnly swear, on the Book of LVL Leadership, to pay it forward."

I laughed and said, "That's better than yes."

"Are you sure there's not one more lesson you want to share? Just for old time's sake?"

"Okay, one more for the road." I took a swig of my beer and began. "My last lesson is about taking control of your future. I have worked with many clients over the course of my career and one of the things that I have learned from some of the best leaders is that one must decide to either move over, move up, or move on."

Justin stopped to write it down in his notebook. "Move over, move up, or move on," he repeated.

"When you stay stagnant, it means that you are either marking time or taking an opportunity away from someone else," I explained. "For example, how many great leaders have we seen who have, shall we say, overstayed their welcome, only to have their successes or careers either washed away or worse yet, end in disaster? I'm not talking about the person who is resigning, retiring, or leaving in a short period of time, but rather the leader who no longer leads, retains the title and office and has stopped developing themselves or their staff."

"Yikes, that sounds like one of the worst things someone can do," Justin replied.

"I deeply believe that once someone is no longer pushing the ball forward, so to speak, it's time for them to step aside and give someone else the opportunity to run with the ball. Everyone has a responsibility to recognize that time when it comes," I said. "So when that time comes for you, hand the ball off to the people you've invested all your leadership in, okay?"

"There's no better way to pay it forward, is there?" Justin asked.

"Exactly!" I said.

There was a moment of silence and then Justin replied, "Bogie, I want to thank you. It's hard to believe that it has almost been a year since we first met. Yet it seems like I have known you my whole life. You appeared out of nowhere when I was at my lowest and took the time to talk with me and remind me that I do have a great deal to offer. It was such a pleasure learning from you."

"The pleasure was mine, Justin," I said.

"Before we sign off, can I offer you one piece of advice?" he asked.

"Oh, how the tides have turned!" I replied. "Of course, I'd love to hear it."

"Earlier, when I swore on the Book of LVL Leadership, I was only half joking," he said.

I gave him a curious look. "What do you mean?"

"I think you should write it," he said.

I still wasn't getting it. "Write what?"

"Write a book! About leadership," Justin said, his voice rising.

I froze as a feeling of excitement washed over me. I thought about all the notes I had been taking on my phone since the moment Maya told me to save them there. I'd actually pulled them into a document on my computer. I'd been adding to it for months, not really knowing why but feeling like I had to do it.

Maybe this was the reason. Maybe this was my next project—and another way to pay it forward.

"Do you think anyone would want to read it?" I asked Justin.

"Yes," Justin said, smiling. "Everyone needs a friend like you, Bogie. Just promise you'll sign a copy of it for me."

And that's exactly what I did, about one year later.

Justin waited in line at the local bookstore for an hour to shake my hand at my launch event. He marked the page he wanted me to sign with his new business card, which read:

Justin Rodriguez
Executive Vice President

Bogie's Notes

➲ Becoming complacent at work not only robs you of your potential, but it keeps a more motivated colleague from moving up.

➲ If you become stagnant, it's time to make a change or move on.

➲ You may still have your title and corner office, but once you've stopped developing, you're no longer a leader.

About the Author

Chris Boguslaw began his career in the Human Capital and Employee Engagement/Development fields while serving in the U.S. Army. He continues to fuel his passion for improving employee and organizational performance today.

Chris and Debbie Boguslaw

A graduate of the Pennsylvania State University, with a Master's of Education degree in instructional systems design, Chris was part of the select "Mobile Training Assist Team" (MTAT) working with the newly created U.S. Department of Homeland Security, Transportation Security Administration (TSA), tasked with training staff to ensure the safety of cargo and passenger air travel after the tragic events of 9/11.

Additionally, he was responsible for managing both training and administrative operations while employed at the U.S. Department of Housing and Urban Development, Philadelphia Homeownership Center, and with the TSA at Philadelphia International Airport.

Chris has served as a part-time adjunct faculty member at Gwynedd-Mercy University, where he has taught various management-related topics for master's, bachelor, and associate degree programs.

He is a highly sought-after presenter and facilitator where his workshops focus on employee engagement, leadership development, communication skills, team building, and customer service.

Chris and his wife, Debbie, reside in Harleysville, Pennsylvania, where they enjoy spending time with their family and friends, bicycling, and traveling.

Acknowledgments

It has been said time and time again, in one form or another, that "no one achieves their goals alone." That couldn't be more true with the completion of this book. I may have put the words on paper, but it was only because I was fortunate enough to be surrounded by loving and caring family, friends, mentors, and co-workers. Thank you.

To everyone who took the time to talk with me about management and leadership, thank you. As you read through this book, I hope you will recognize some of our discussions and know that "I heard you!"

The thought of writing a book is fun, exciting, and exhilarating! However, for me, the reality of actually writing a book was both one of the most difficult things I have ever done and one of the most rewarding. Had it not been for the good fortune of working with such an amazing editor and published author, Claudia Gabel Lindvall, I am sure I would still be staring at a lot of blank pages and talking about finishing my book one day. Claudia, thank you for using your "red pen" in such a kind way. In addition, your insight, suggestions, and encouraging words were key to getting me to the "finish line." You are a master at your profession. Thank you!

To my parents and my children, thank you. There just are not enough words to even try to describe how appreciative I am for all you have done for me.

The person I would like to thank the most for this book becoming a reality is my wife, Deb, whose counsel, advice, suggestions, patience, and words of encouragement made the difference and is what kept me motivated to keep writing. Thanks, Deb!

ABOUT 'TEAM BOGIE'
Training and Organizational Development Consultants, LLC

"**Team Bogie**" helps individuals, teams, and organizations by identifying solutions to human behaviors and process-oriented barriers that get in the way of organizations achieving optimal performance.

We would love the opportunity to discuss any challenges your organization is experiencing and partner together to identify solutions. Training/services that we provide include:

◆ Facilitating Retreats

◆ Keynote Presentations

◆ Custom and "Off the Shelf" Training programs, including but not limited to:

  ◇ Communication Skills

  ◇ Time Management

  ◇ Leadership Development

  ◇ Team/Individual Accountability and Expectations

  ◇ Team-building Programs

To learn more about these programs and other solutions, please contact us at: **www.teambogie.com**